BECOMING
WORTHY
ANCESTORS

T0366701

ARCHIVE,
PUBLIC DELIBERATION AND IDENTITY
IN SOUTH AFRICA

Edited by
Xolela Mangcu

To forgotten histories

Published in South Africa by:
Wits University Press
1 Jan Smuts Avenue
Johannesburg
www.witspress.co.za

First published 2011
ISBN 978-1-86814-532-4

Edited by Monica Seeber
Cover design by The Library
Book design and layout by The Library
Printed and bound by Ultra Litho (Pty) Limited

CONTENTS

PREFACE

XOLELA MANGCU

In 2006 my colleague Carolyn Hamilton invited me to be a fellow in the Constitution of Public Intellectual Life Project at Wits University. The aim of the fellowship was to deepen and broaden discussions around the role of the archive in South Africa. I took up this question in relation to the making of a new South African identity asking: why does it matter that nations should care for their archives, and that they should develop a sense of shared identity? And why should these processes take place in the public domain? How could nations possibly speak about a shared sense of identity in pluralistic societies where individuals and groups also have multiple identities? And how, as Hamilton asks in her essay in this volume, can such conversations be given relevance in public discussions of reconciliation and development in South Africa?

In order to problematise these questions I thought it would be useful to invite outside scholars to join local commentators in a series of public deliberations on the contestations of archive and identity that often characterise new nations. The outside scholars I invited are regarded as leading authorities on questions of national identity and archive in the world.

In my essay, which opens the discussion in this book, I describe as evidentiary genocide the denial of the role of the Black Consciousness Movement and the Pan Africanist movement in the narrative of democracy in South Africa. In fact, denial is only part of the story. Even more dangerous has been the 're-presentation' of black consciousness as a nativist movement – quite the furthest from what it was, and from Steve Biko's description of black identity in strictly political (as opposed to biological) terms. Aimé Césaire once said that 'blackness is historical and there is nothing biological about it.'[1] The exclusion and then 're-presentation' of black consciousness from the public archive has had deleterious effects on our political culture, particularly in terms of how we think about identity, progress and development – a point that Carolyn Hamilton also makes in her chapter, which closes this volume.

In his chapter, Ntongela Masilela seeks to redress what Hamilton calls 'the neglect and negation of the archive of black intellectual history'. Masilela has put together the most comprehensive online archive on black intellectual history, giving truth to Edward Said's argument about how the Internet has altered the inert concept of the archive we have inherited from the past. Titled the New African Movement, the website brings to life the contributions of nineteenth and twentieth century black intellectuals such as Tiyo Soga, John Tengo Jabavu, WB Rubusana, Magema Fuze, SEK Mqhayi, WW Gqoba, Sol Plaatje, RV Selope Thema, HIE Dhlomo and Benedict Vilakazi. While Masilela's primary motivation is to redress the negation of the archive of black intellectual history, his website is also racially and ethnically quite eclectic. It also includes scholars, writers and political figures with varying political and intellectual outlooks – from nineteenth century missionaries such as John William Colenso and Alexander Kerr to Mohandas Gandhi, Clement Martyn Doke, Fatima Meer, Alex La Guma, Peter Abrahams and many others. Masilela's essay is an example of what is possible when scattered materials are convened as an archive. In mapping the transmission lines of the circulation of ideas among the New Africans, Masilela uses his web archives to make a contribution to the reconfiguring of the 'archive'. Later in this volume Carolyn Hamilton describes the archive as 'the circumscribed body of knowledge of the past that is historically determined as that which is available for us to draw on when thinking about the past'. In his chapter, Masilela gives close attention to the formation of intellectual constellations and draws our attention to the processes by which the intellectuals of what became known as the New African Movement sought, as early as the mid-nineteenth century, to imagine a new African modernity. Their modernity incorporated the African past in ways very different from the intellectual texts of European modernity, effectively using the new newspapers of the time as the setting for public deliberation on African modernity. Masilela's essay in this volume emphasises a long tradition of problematisation, whether of the ideas of tradition and chieftaincy, the popular and the classical, or of modernity and collective democratic leadership. It is, in that sense, a much needed antidote to nativist essentialism.

The late Frederick van Zyl Slabbert takes up the theme of the use of the past to suit present-day ideological interests, and puts the accent on individual notions of identity. According to Slabbert, the past is being selectively drawn upon in South Africa today to establish Africanism in an exclusive sense as the new dominant ideology. Taking as his starting point Thabo Mbeki's 1996 'I am an African' speech, Slabbert offers a critique of the concept of 'African-ness' as a value-laden ideological concept of nationality, ethnicity and race. While Mbeki's speech contained an inclusive vision of the African, the current political climate makes it clear that a coloured, Indian or white person is not generally seen as an African. Slabbert takes his cue from the so-called 'National Question' outlined in the ANC journal *Umrabulo* No. 23 and put before the ANC National Congress in June 2005, which is about 'the liberation of Blacks in general and Africans in particular'. To Slabbert, the racialisation of public policy through affirmative action and black economic empowerment programmes go against the non-racial idealism in Mbeki's speech. In his view, the moment one moves away from a geographical definition of the African one enters a world of ideological agendas and value judgments. He asserts that he is African because he is from Africa, because he grew up and lives in South Africa and because he has a South African identity document. He concludes on an uncompromising note: by inventing the past to suit current ideological pursuits, it becomes more difficult to avoid repeating mistakes in dealing with the problems of the present. Slabbert's essay thus prompts us to consider how an exclusionary discourse of Africanism can work to alienate significant sections of the population. Equally, Slabbert's contribution draws our attention to the challenges that face white South Africans as they grapple with their African identity and in assuming their responsibilities as citizens who can enter spaces of public deliberation as individuals committed to the problematisation of identity.

Martin Bernal's challenge is the critical excavation of the archive to back claims of human achievement. I have known Martin Bernal from my student days at Cornell University in the early to mid-1990s. Anyone interested in the role of Africa in the world would have been attuned to the heated debates that came in the wake of the publication of *Black Athena: The Afroasiatic Roots of Western Civilization*. The *Black Athena* series is now widely regarded as a watershed in the study of African origins of Western civilisation, effectively challenging the way European scholarship has denied and suppressed Africa's contribution to the West. In the first two volumes of *Black Athena*, Bernal presented archaeological and philosophical evidence of Africa's contribution. In the third and final volume (of which his lecture provided a preview), Bernal offers linguistic evidence of Africa's contribution to Greek civilisation. He argues that since about 40 per cent of Greek vocabulary is of Egyptian origin one does not have to be a racial nativist to make and sustain the claim that Africa was the fount of European civilisation. This argument is likely to spark as much controversy as did the previous two volumes, which attracted the criticism of those who said they were methodologically flawed; the praises of those who felt vindicated in their claims of African civilisation; the disapproval of those who argue that black scholars have made similar points before; and the outright opposition of conservatives such as Mary Leifkowitz who edited a critical volume on Bernal entitled *Not Out of Africa: How Afrocentrism Became an Excuse to Teach Myth as History*. Leifkowitz, a well-known classisist and conservative activist ironically accuses Bernal of lack of objectivity and of presenting mythology as history. But Bernal concedes that all intellectual work is ultimately political. Bernal refuses to be co-opted by purists of the 'out of Africa' variety or yield to the criticism of the 'not out of Africa' variety. 'I am the enemy of purity,' he famously declared in his lecture, arguing that ancient Egypt was just as diverse as is human society but that there can be no questioning that Egypt is the vortex out of which early Greek philosophers were educated and inspired. Bernal argues that Egypt's role was a widely acknowledged fact until the rise of racism and anti-Semitism in nineteenth century Europe. This was left out of the colonial archive so as to provide new ideological underpinnings for modern racism and colonial rule.

Pumla Gqola argues against the popular conception that there is an absence of women intellectuals in the public domain, and suggests that in looking for the intellectual contributions of black women we should go beyond the nightly television news to other outlets and publications in which women intellectuals are actively involved. She also suggests that the best way to understand black women's intellectual contribution is to read against the grain of the inherited archive – instead of looking at women's intellectual history as a linear, teleological development we should pay close attention to some of the contradictions that have emerged and that may not fit a singular narrative. For example, while it is often assumed that people like Phyllis Ntantala, Epainette Mbeki and many others were simply following and supporting their husbands in the liberation struggle, Gqola demonstrates that many of these partnerships were forged by women and men who came independently into the liberation movement. The narrative of the 'supportive' spouse has to be critically examined.

Kwame Anthony Appiah traces the modern nation state back to 1648, when the Treaty of Westphalia divided the Holy Roman Empire into a collection of largely German speaking nation-states each with its own sovereign. Something more, however, was required for the modern nation state to emerge, and that quality is what Johann Friedrich Herder has called its '*volksgeist*' or national ethnos. Appiah problematises the idea of a common heritage or a common 'national ethnos' that often informs the formation of the nation state. The idea of a common heritage is sustained not only by denying the reality that individuals and communities have different recollections of the past, but also that they choose what to remember on the basis of present-day political exigencies. The production of the past, and the very archives out of which that past is produced, is always a matter of present-day decisions and choices, of exercises of power and acts of resistance: 'In truth, national history is a question of what we choose to remember, not just in the sense of which facts we use for our public purposes, but equally in the sense that we choose which facts actually count as ours.' Appiah invites us then to look closely at how we decide which facts will count as ours, pointing out that how we make those decisions determines our future. 'South African identity, like that of any living nation, is a work in progress. Its meaning will repose in an archive that remains to be written.' He also counsels that ultimately it is not nations that remember, but individuals who play that important role in the making of the archive. The remembering, however, does not take place in a vacuum, for the recognition of individuality is not the same thing as individualism; people live in the context of relationships with others who collectively shape their identities, with the state, educational institutions and the media also playing a crucial role in the making of identity. Appiah argues that nationality is only one aspect of an individual identity. Ultimately, people are more than their identities, they also have identity interests, which can either be fulfilled or undermined by public policy.

Benedict Anderson is one of the world's foremost scholars of nationalism, and his work *Imagined Communities*[2] is arguably the most frequently cited book on nationalism and national identity. Drawing on his more recent work, the article *On the Goodness of Nations*, Anderson urges us to consider afresh the nature of the social glue that brings nations together, to what extent it is squeezed out of the past, and the extent to which it can be set in the present so as to imagine a collective future. If Appiah is less sanguine about collective imagination, Anderson draws on Max Weber's argument that we ought to be 'worthy ancestors' – hence the title of this book – to the future unborn, the future that thus imposes obligations on the present to be preserved and actively to cultivate the goodness of the nation. The second source of this goodness of nations comes from obligations imposed on the present by the past or the innocent dead. Anderson notes the way in which the nation rummages through its archive to find worthy ancestors from its past, and embarks on continuous processes of memorialisation. The third source of this goodness lies in the present, and is particularly about how the nation treats its children as 'innocent' by, *inter alia*, not allowing them to vote, which absolves them from the atrocities that characterise the life of the modern nation (of which genocide is the most chilling). In *The Age of Extremes*, Eric Hobsbawm argues that modern technology turned the killing and maiming of large numbers of people into impersonal warfare: 'so the world accustomed itself to the compulsory expulsion and killing on an astronomical scale, phenomena so unfamiliar that new words had to be invented for them "stateless (apatride) and genocide".'[3] For Anderson, the preoccupation of social groups and nations is not happiness in heaven or torment in hell: it is the quite earthly possibility of extinction through genocide. Anderson believes that the goodness of nations, which can be expressed through shame at the behavior of one's nation towards others, serves as an antidote to such destructive forces.

Carolyn Hamilton's essay goes to the crux of the matter, which is how the archive becomes the source of authority for making claims about the past in order to justify present-day actions and policies. Hamilton makes a useful distinction between 'archive' and 'archives'. 'Archive' is an epistemological concept that circumscribes what evidence from the past is considered legitimate or is to be included in the narrative of the nation. 'Archives' refers to the actual storehouse of collected materials from the past. Both archive and archives constitute what Hamilton describes as 'the archive.'

Logically, then, the archive is a source of contestation, and this is precisely why public deliberation is vital to discussions of the archive. Hamilton notes that the South African government has convened a Habermasian public sphere through public institutions and policies, particularly around the three themes of reconciliation, development and identity politics. However, this public sphere is equally inflected with power, which leads to 'the exiling of unwanted memories', various forms of cultural conservatism and nativism and the corralling and silencing of dissentient voices. Not only is the archive compromised but there also tends to be a bias towards heritage discourses over archival ones. At the heart of the chapter is a call for new archival discourses informed by the principle of public accessibility and an ongoing responsibility of citizens to engage with the archive in both its epistemological political sense and as the storehouse of materials from the past.

Hamilton identifies areas where the engagement with the archive should take place. For example, she argues that there is in South Africa a palpable hunger for literature, whether in the form of novels or memoirs. These forms of affective expression need an engagement with the archive – but an engagement that is outside the evidentiary paradigm and practices of much archival work: 'the vitality of discourse in these areas is because they are regarded as creative and as being concerned with affect, as opposed to reason, evidence and history'. Literature often involves the telling of multiple truths, and thus tends to leave the formal archive and its certitudes wanting. Hamilton also calls for greater engagement between the archive and the political arena. This is important if we are to avoid the insider/outsider narratives that have had chilling effects, sometimes even involving genocide.

The participants in the original series of deliberations took up my questions in a range of different ways. Some of the contributions are distinctly scholarly, others polemical, invocative or recuperative. I have retained the unevenness of the original series in this volume in order to ensure that the significance of each distinctive response is registered on the terms in which it was offered. The chapters also retain the colloquial and accessible format of the public lecture in an effort to provide effective entry points into the various authors' larger, and sometimes more esoteric, bodies of work. This book is not without limitations. One of those is the tentative nature of the essays, particularly those written by foreign scholars, a quality that is far more honourable than the presumptuousness that has characterised much of the writing about Africa. As Kwame Anthony Appiah puts it: 'South African identity, like that of any living nation, is a work in progress. Its meaning will repose in an archive that remains to be written.' The critical message of this book is that the writing of that archive must be an integral part of our public life, involving a continual opening and democratisation of the already convened public sphere through ongoing public deliberation.

ACKNOWLEDGEMENTS

I could not have undertaken this work without fellowship support from Atlantic Philanthropies and funding for the lectures from the Ford Foundation. Throughout this process, Carolyn Hamilton provided her unconditional support and motivation, always insisting that we needed to 'open up the space' for public intellectual life at a time when it was under considerable threat of closure. This book would not have been possible without her continual prodding and unmatched intellectual rigour. Oliver Barstow and Lenore Longwe ensured that the organisational machinery was always in place for the smooth running of the lectures, and that I submitted changes to the manuscript on time. And of course I should like to thank the members of the public who attended the lectures. The discussions were an enactment of the democratic culture we should all endeavour to achieve – free, open and vibrant.

EVIDENTIARY GENOCIDE: INTERSECTIONS OF RACE, POWER AND THE ARCHIVE

1

XOLELA MANGCU

MEMORY, POWER AND NATION BUILDING

Central to this book are questions of memory, archive, identity and public deliberation. These chapters consider why it matters that nations should care for their archives, and why those archives should inform discussions about a sense of shared identity. I deliberately distinguish between shared identity and common identity, for while we cannot speak of a common identity and experiences, even within a group of people, the concept of 'shared identity', by definition, suggests the existence of multiple individuals and groups who have a stake in the continued existence of the nation.

But this book does not seek to settle age-old debates about shared identity in pluralist societies. Its aim is to highlight how the archive is often employed to make certain identity claims and, in the process, to privilege certain identities' histories over others. At its worst, this claim-making leads to the genocide of individuals and groups in the name of the nation or, conversely, the genocide of the nation in the name of groups. As Benedict Anderson puts it in his chapter: 'No nation looks forward to happiness in Heaven, or torment in Hell. What it fears is the quite earthly: the possibility of extinction through genocide.' To use a cliché, memory becomes the weapon, quite literally.

Archbishop Desmond Tutu has explained the role that memory plays in affirming individual and group identity – but also as a weapon of extinction:

> My identity is linked very intimately to my memory ...
> What I know is what I remember, and that helps to make

1

me who I am. Nations are built through sharing experiences, memories, and a history. That is why people have often tried to destroy their enemies by destroying their histories, their memories, that which gives them an identity.[1]

The physical genocide of groups and nations is thus often preceded by what I would call evidentiary genocide. Public deliberation around issues of identity and archive becomes both the means and the end of interrogating those identity claims, and of exposing their use in the service of power.

In her chapter, Carolyn Hamilton makes a distinction between archive as the epistemological and political frame that shapes how we approach the past and archives as the actual collections of materials about the past. My introductory chapter focuses more on the former – the manner in which formative aspects of our history have been left out of the historical narrative of the nation, and the implications thereof for developing a sense of shared identity. More specifically, I demonstrate how, under the leadership of former president Thabo Mbeki, South Africa's ruling party, the African National Congress, appropriated the language of the Black Consciousness and Pan Africanist movements while disfiguring the role of those movements in the struggle for liberation, with specific and real consequences for how we think about development.

One of the great illustrations of the costs of forgetting is captured in this opening vignette from Milan Kundera's novel *The Book of Laughter and Forgetting*:

In February 1948, the communist leader Klement Gottwald stepped out on the balcony of a Baroque palace in Prague to harangue hundreds of thousands of citizens massed in Old Town Square. Gottwald was flanked by comrades, with Clementis standing close to him. It was snowing and cold, and Gottwald was bareheaded. Bursting with solicitude, Clementis took off his fur hat and set it on Gottwald's head. The propaganda section made hundreds of thousands of copies of the photograph taken on the balcony where Gottwald, in a fur hat and surrounded by his comrades, spoke to the people. On that balcony the history of Communist Bohemia began. Every child knew that photograph, from seeing it on posters and in schoolbooks and museums. Four years later Clementis was charged with treason and hanged. The propaganda section immediately made him vanish from history and, of course, from all photographs. Ever since, Gottwald has been alone on the balcony. Where Clementis stood, there is only the bare palace wall. Nothing remains of Clementis but the fur hat on Gottswald head.[2]

South Africa's various liberation movements became the fur hat on the ruling party's head as it dressed itself in nationalist garb in the early 2000s. If Thabo Mbeki emerged as our metaphorical Gottwald, then Pan Africanist and Black Consciousness leaders such as Robert Sobukwe and Steve Biko became our metaphorical Clementis, although it is hard to associate Sobukwe or Biko with the obsequiousness of a Clementis. In one of the early acts of historical erasure, Jacob Zuma, then deputy president of the ANC, claimed, in an article in *City Press*, that the ANC had masterminded the June 1976 uprisings. Long before my intellectual interest in the role of the archive in nation building, I utilised the ANC's own archives to refute Zuma's claim. I retrieved an article that appeared in the ANC's mouthpiece *Sechaba* barely a month after the uprisings. The publication literally labelled the 1976 uprisings a mark of adventurism and concluded that, unlike the generation of Mandela, Tambo, Sisulu and other Youth Leaguers of the 1950s, the youth of 1976 lacked a sound political direction and leadership.[3] I argued then, as I do now, that the ANC, while dominant, should be careful not to suggest that the history of this country can be understood only through its lens.

More recently, the leader of the ANC Youth League, Julius Malema, stated on public television that the historic events of Sharpeville on 21 March 1960 were not organised by the PAC as had been generally acknowledged, but by the omnipresent ANC. This created so much uproar that PAC youth leaders threatened Malema's life, demonstrating once again the deadly business of memory. Some of us have taken the more persuasive route of reminding our society of the role that individuals such as Biko and Sobukwe played in the construction of our political identities, and I did as much in responding to Malema's distortion of history.[4] We have taken it upon ourselves to protect their philosophies from the vulgarisation of present-day nationalism in the service of power. As Kundera puts it: ' ... the struggle of man against power is the struggle of memory against forgetting'.[5]

THE COLLUSION OF THE MEDIA

Evidentiary genocide has not been the exclusive monopoly of the ruling party and the state. The power to shape memories also operates in more horizontal capillarial ways and the forgetting takes place in civil society when, for example, powerful institutions such as the media privilege certain histories over others; if the ANC saw itself as 'the sole authentic voice' of South Africans, the local and international media played no small part in that representation. Even if we concede that other political movements were on the decline, it is evident that the media abetted the glorification of one particular movement over others and the privileging of one vision over others. The reason for the media bias would most likely be that the ANC's philosophy of non-racialism was far less threatening than the radicalism of these other movements; the media played a particularly critical role in the presentation of Mbeki as the sophisticated black intellectual who was the voice of reason. Again, the media was actively involved in the way in which Nelson Mandela – and, to a lesser extent, the 'terrorist' Oliver Tambo – became the icon of the new South Africa. The choice of certain icons over others could be seen in the furore over the re-naming of Johannesburg International Airport as Oliver Tambo International Airport; for white South Africans, Oliver Tambo was the 'terrorist' while Mandela was the one who forgave them and absolved them of any historical responsibility.

In its glorification and privileging of the ANC, the media forgot that it was only at its conference in Mogorogoro in 1969 that membership was opened to whites, and that it was only at the Kabwe Conference in 1985 that whites were allowed to hold leadership positions. It could be argued therefore that Mbeki was taking the ANC to an earlier self that the media had wilfully ignored.

But beyond the matter of plurality why would it be substantively important to include the story of other movements in the making of our nation? Let us take black consciousness as an example.

THE RISE AND FALL OF BLACK CONSCIOUSNESS

In 1960, the apartheid government outlawed the main political organisations in the black community, the African National Congress and the Pan Africanist Congress. The PAC had broken ranks with the ANC in 1959 in opposition to the latter's adoption of the Freedom Charter, a document which stated that the land belonged to both blacks and whites. To radical nationalists within the ANC, the mother body had lost its claim as the custodian of African nationalism. The PAC also argued that the ANC was dominated by white liberals and communists. The Black Consciousness Movement emerged in the late 1960s to fill the political vacuum left by the banning of these two organisations. In many ways, the new movement was close to the PAC in its radical nationalism and in its assertion of racial identity as a weapon of struggle. However, while the PAC did not completely bar white membership, the Black Consciousness Movement excluded it completely. As Robert Fatton argues, the PAC's inspiration was the continent itself whereas the inspiration of the Black Consciousness Movement were the Third World political and intellectual movements.[6]

Here is how Barney Pityana captured the impact of these political and intellectual currents on the movement's founder, Steve Biko:

Black Consciousness for him was moulded by a diversity of intellectual forces and fountains: from the liberation history of South Africa, the Pan Africanism of Kwame Nkrumah, the African nationalism of Jomo Kenyatta, the negritude of the west African scholars like Leopold Sadar Senghor, Aimé Césaire and others in Paris. Biko taught himself a political understanding of religion in Africa. He devoured John Mbiti. Ali Mazrui. Basil Davidson. He understood the critical writings of Walter Rodney and he interpreted Frantz Fanon. He laid his hands on some philosophical writings like Jean Paul Sartre and made ready use of some philosophical concepts like syllogism in logic and dialectical materialism in Marxist political thought. All this by a young medical student.[7]

This movement lasted for the better part of the 1970s, reaching its high water mark with the 1976 student uprisings. Steve Biko was killed by the apartheid security police in 1977, and all the black consciousness organisations were banned in the following month.

Yet another lull occurred in the late 1970s as former black consciousness leaders sought to regroup under the leadership of the Azanian People's Organisation. But it was also precisely during this period that movements sympathetic to the non-racialism of the ANC emerged, culminating in the formation of the United Democratic Front. It is extremely difficult to pinpoint the founders of political movements, as often an idea will have circulated for a while in the community before finding its most articulate spokesperson – who then takes on the title of the founder. The person most closely associated with the formation of the UDF was Allan Boesak, later a prominent member of the ANC when it was unbanned.

The UDF took the initiative from a weakened Black Consciousness Movement and made no bones about its support for the ANC and its philosophy of non-racialism. This multiracial body dominated South African politics throughout the 1980s. When the UDF was banned, it was replaced by the Mass

Democratic Movement, which consisted of a combination of mass action and underground military organisation. Elsewhere, I have described the transition from black consciousness to the mass mobilisation of the 1980s in the following terms:

> Whereas the Black Consciousness Movement had concentrated on inward-looking strategies of community development in preparation for an idealised non-racial order, the new movements directed the struggle almost exclusively outwardly. Impatient with the steady pace and institution building of the 1970s, the 'young lions' of the 1980s brought a dizzying urgency to the situation. Seeking to make the country ungovernable, this generation's emphasis was more on mobilisation of the masses than on organisation and institution building.[8]

The changeover from the dominance of the philosophy of black consciousness to the non-racialism of the UDF and the ANC was violent, laying claim to many lives as the two movements competed for ideological hegemony in the black community. And thus were planted the seeds for the kind of militarism we would come to witness, especially among young people in the 1990s. The talk of killing to protect ANC president Jacob Zuma thus has antecedents that go back to the youth violence of the 1980s. While many people have rightfully deplored ANC Youth League President Julius Malema's statement to kill to defend Zuma, the reality is that it is a language that many young, hopeless and marginalised youth find seductive.

The UDF/ANC alliance ultimately prevailed and imposed the hegemony of non-racialism in the liberation struggle throughout the 1980s and early 1990s, and this in turn influenced much of the political discourse until the Mandela years. Mandela did not pay much attention to the political culture within the black community, investing much of his time in a process of building relations with white people and the international community.

THE COSTS OF FORGETTING: IDENTITY AND DEVELOPMENT IN THE
NEW ERA

One of the more perceptive observations of changing political
attitudes in the black community after apartheid came from
Mandela's biographer, Anthony Sampson:

> In his first months as president, he enjoyed a brilliant hon-
> eymoon, particularly with white South Africans, to whom
> this tolerant old man came as a wondrous relief ... at the
> end of the first hundred days in office the *Financial Times*
> could find no whites who had a bad word for him. It was
> a normality which carried its own dangers, as black mili-
> tants saw the revolution betrayed, and younger ANC lead-
> ers including Thabo Mbeki knew they must make reforms
> which would offend the whites.[9]

Mbeki adopted the once 'discredited' Pan Africanist and black
consciousness themes of African unity and identity for South
Africa and spoke increasingly of an African renaissance and
the themes of black self-determination that were at the heart
of black consciousness. He also admitted leading Pan Africanist and black consciousness figures to his inner circle and cabinet. There were, however, two central contradictions in Mbeki's appeal to black consciousness.

First, there was the emergence of a nativist, essentialist
discourse coming from Mbeki and his closest advisors. Even
though black consciousness had always been an exclusivist
movement, it had never adopted an essentialist approach to
identity; one of the great achievements of the liberation movement was the manner in which identities were de-essentialised
and given a political meaning, and blackness for example was
never constructed as simply a matter of skin colour or biology.
For Steve Biko, blackness was always a matter of consciousness and identification, hence the movement's description of
black people as 'all those who are by law and tradition dis-
criminated against, and identify themselves as a unit towards

the realisation of their aspirations' The nativist, essentialist reading of black consciousness themes was part of a trend of appeals to racial solidarity among Southern African leaders. Like Robert Mugabe in Zimbabwe, Mbeki saw in radical racial nationalism a way of mobilising black support against critics. For example he castigated black critics of his government as 'foot lickers of the white man' and he suggested that white critics, irrespective of their political pedigree, were acting out racist stereotypes about Africans as corrupt. Veteran ANC leader Jeremy Cronin was reprimanded by ANC leader Dumisani Makhaye after he said there was a process of Zanu-fication taking place within the ANC (a clear reference to the authoritarianism of Zimbabwe's ZANU-PF). What was instructive was the racialised nature of the reprimand. And the essentialism lies in the fact that it is Cronin's whiteness that disqualified him from speaking about Zimbabwe, not his ideas or values. In other words Cronin's detractors were saying, 'it's a black thing you can't understand'.[10] Mbeki and his cohorts were effectively re-presenting the black consciousness critique of white racism as a nativist reduction of political consciousness to skin colour.

One of Mbeki's supporters, Ronald Suresh Roberts, wrote a book, *Fit to Govern, The Native Intelligence of Thabo Mbeki*,[11] which castigates every white critic of government as a racist, and every black critic a lackey of the white system. Mbeki's supporters tried to rewrite Steve Biko into history as a racial essentialist . But Biko had warned about this negative obsession with whiteness : 'Blacks have had enough experience as objects of racism not to wish to turn the tables. While it may be relevant now to talk about black in relation to white, we must not make this our preoccupation, for it can be a negative exercise. As we proceed further towards the achievement of our goals let us talk more about ourselves and our struggle and less about whites.'[12]

But is it possible that Biko himself was an essentialist and that Mbeki's race discourse was merely an extension of that essentialism? For example, in his chapter 'Some African Cultural Concepts' in *I Write What I Like*, Biko writes about Africans as having a collectivist culture as opposed to the more individualistic culture of the West. Dismissing Biko as an essentialist on that basis would require us to dismiss all descriptions of social and cultural behaviour, for history does inform people's behaviour and values. CB Macpherson's work on 'possessive individualism' as the foundational ethic of Western market societies is a case in point.[13] Benjamin Barber also describes Western liberalism as a politics ' ... which enthrones not only the individual but the individual defined by his perimeters, his parapets and his entrenched solitude. Politics is at best a matter of 'let's make a deal', where the states are exclusively private'. Barber further notes that 'in establishing the solitary individual as the model citizen, liberalism short-changed ideas of citizenship and community, and contrived a fictional self so unencumbered by situation and context as to be useful only in challenging the very idea of the political'.[14]

Essentialism occurs when behaviour is attributed to some innate quality that members of a group are said to possess, but Biko never argued that all people with a black skin possessed an innate progressive, let alone radical, political consciousness. In fact, his description of collaborators with the apartheid system as 'non-whites' is proof of the anti-essentialism of his politics. But for one to get a job in the Mbeki era it was sufficient that one had a black skin and pledged fealty to the president.

Biko was of course greatly influenced in his approach to identity by people such as Aimé Césaire – to whom blackness was not a biological identity – and Frantz Fanon, the canonical figure of the times.[15] Nigel Gibson argues that 'Steve Biko was powerfully affected by Fanon's writings',[16] and Biko affirmed this when Gail Gerhart asked him about Third World political leaders who had influenced the movement. 'Much more people like Fanon', Biko replied.[17] Just as Fanon had responded sharply to Sartre's notion that subjectivity was a minor matter, Biko rejected the idea of black consciousness as transitory by positing that black consciousness was a state of mind – a never-ending reach for creative subjectivity – but not a form of racial essentialism of any kind. The second contradiction in

Mbeki's appeal to black consciousness was that even as he was adopting an increasingly nationalist posture he was imposing on the country a technocratic approach to development that was contrary to many of the tenets of self-reliant community development that defined the movement. Even as he signalled a shift to greater emphasis on cultural self-determination, he pushed for conservative economic policies inspired by and designed in cahoots with the World Bank. The government's Growth, Employment and Redistribution Strategy (GEAR) was formulated in partnership with these institutions to the exclusion of the ANC's partners, and the scholar Patrick Bond described Mbeki's strategy as 'talking left and walking right'.[18] Mbeki became Africa's champion on world forums even as he presided over economic policies that intensified unemployment and income inequality in his own country.

Like other identity movements around the world, the Black Consciousness Movement was informed by the post-development discourse of self-reliant development – or what Harry Boyte calls culture making.[19] With the rise of identity movements in the 1970s, freedom and development were no longer merely about inclusion into a pre-existing political and developmental framework defined by Western values. People such as Julius Nyerere, Paolo Freire and Frantz Fanon – many of whose writings in turn influenced Biko – had articulated a more fundamental reshaping of the world to reflect the cultural values and outlook of oppressed people. Development was not merely about consuming what was made available to the poor but was essentially a process of self-determination by utilising the cultural and psychological resources that are present in any given community. However, upon assuming the reins of power the ANC adopted rule by the experts. Public problems could only be solved by ANC-appointed experts, and civic groups were explicitly told to cooperate with the government. After all, was this not the government they had said they wanted? From its inception the ANC government placed emphasis on the quantitative dimension of development: how many houses, water taps and electricity connections would be delivered to the community. Service delivery became the watchword of development.

The epistemological shift in thinking about development was shared by liberals and Marxists alike – inside and outside the ANC. Liberals believed that identity-talk interfered with the role of markets in the allocation of resources. Marxists argued that the politics of identity were merely an expression of false consciousness. This should not be surprising for a modernist, integrationist organisation such as the ANC, founded at the height of the Enlightenment, a period in which scientific rationality and economic development were expected to deliver the human race from backward cultural identities and practices. As Carolyn Hamilton, following Arturo Escobar, notes in her chapter in this volume, 'For much of the second half of the twentieth century, the international discourse about development was essentially that of modernity and was geared towards ensuring the availability of opportunities for modernisation underpinned by appropriate infrastructure and skills'. Hamilton thus urges us to 'unveil the colonial foundations of the order of knowledge ... which define aspects of our society as underdeveloped (the successor term to "primitive")'. I would argue that a retrieval of the thinking and practices of the Black Consciousness Movement would allow us, in Hamilton's words, 'to explore the potential contributions in this post-development era of modes of self-identification and accreditation in the development of self-capability, as well as the possible contributions of inherited practices and local forms of modernity'.

SPEAKING THE TRUTH, PUBLICLY

The point I have been making is that the assemblage of an archive is often characterised by a process of 'selective retrieval', for what is left out of the archive is just as important as what is included. The selective retrieval has real consequences in shaping public consciousness and public policy. We would be fooling ourselves indeed if we imagined that the archive we have now is the only archive we could have ever had, just as we would be fooling ourselves if we imagined that the identities we now have are the only identities we could have ever had. As Jean Francis Bayart argues in *The Illusion of Identity*: ' ... there is no natural identity capable of imposing itself on man by the very nature of things ... there are only strategies based on identity'.[20] The strategic use of identity involves a great deal of what Benedict Anderson describes as the dialectic process of remembering and forgetting in imagining the nation. This dialectic makes it all the more imperative for citizens of a country not to remember their history only in the privacy of their own homes or groups. They need to speak publicly about their past and its implications for the development of a representative national archive and a sense of shared identity and development.

Writing about truth and politics, Hannah Arendt describes how archives can be manipulated to tell a story in a particular way: 'Facts, like the materials that make up an archive must first be picked out of a chaos of sheer happenings ... and then be fitted into a story that can be told only in a certain perspective, which has nothing to do with the original occurrence.'[21] Arendt writes about how politicians in the Soviet Union intervened to re-write the archive and in the process erased certain individuals from history. The erasure could in turn lead to death: 'When Trotsky learned that he had never played a role in the Russian Revolution he must have known that his death warrant had been signed.'[22] Stalin ordered the re-assemblage of the archives in 1935. In those archives were the manuscripts and speeches of all the leaders that he wanted erased from history, as well as the minutes and correspondences of the various official bodies, from the Party congresses, to the central committee meetings, to anthologies on Marxism, that were out of keeping with his own view of the world.[23] In short, Stalin was involved in nothing less than evidentiary genocide. Gianna Pomata describes how Stalin systematically erased the memory of populism in Russia. The peasants and the populists had existed side by side with Marxists in nineteenth century

Russia – the former espousing the peasant economy and the latter scientific Marxism based on industrialisation. But for Stalin the populists were an impediment and the solution was evidentiary genocide:

> All the men, ideas, and journals associated with neo-Populism disappeared in 1935-36. The security measures adopted by Stalin dealt not only with the living but also with the dead: even the editing of the works of historical leaders stopped. An impenetrable silence fell on Populism not only in the political debate, but even in Soviet historiography.[24]

Arendt was just as concerned with the public's collusion in the concealment of truth, even over what she called 'publicly known facts'. She did not question that states had to have their secrets, or the need for government classification of information; what concerned her the most was the self-censorship that led people to be afraid to speak about even 'publicly known facts' or 'unwelcome factual truths'. As one of Kundera's characters puts it when he is reprimanded by his comrades for being careless in keeping minutes and correspondence about their meetings: 'We're not doing anything that violates the constitution. To hide and feel guilty would be the beginning of defeat.'[25]

Vaclav Havel, the Czech playwright, poet and politician, also depicts the impact of self-censorship in the Eastern bloc, describing how the manager of a fruit and vegetable shop wakes up every day to put up, among the carrots and the onions, a banner that reads: 'Workers of the world unite'. He does this because 'if he were to refuse he could be in trouble. He could be reproached for not having the proper "decoration" in his window; someone might even accuse him of disloyalty. He does it because these things must be done if one is to get along in life.'[26] Havel argues that this is a world in which people literally and actively 'divest themselves of their innermost identity by convincing themselves that the truth is the lie and the lie the truth'.[27] This is possible because 'each person succumbs to a profane trivialisation of his or her inherent humanity, and to utilitarianism. In everyone there is some willingness to merge with the anonymous crowd and to flow comfortably along with it down the river of a pseudo-life. This is much more than a simple conflict between two identities. It is something far worse: it is a challenge to the very notion of identity itself.' But Havel also describes how the shop manager wakes up one day and decides not to put up the banner of deception. He stops speaking in hushed tones, and finds his real voice in the din of the anonymous crowd. Friends initially look the other way or cross the street when he comes along. He becomes a social outcast, the disloyal one. But he persists in telling the truth, and one by one the banners begin to come down. This is what Zackie Achmat did when he encouraged South Africans to pull down the banners of deception around HIV/AIDS. Before we knew it we had a national movement mobilised against Mbeki's denialism of HIV/AIDS, leading ultimately to a Constitutional Court ruling forcing his government to extend medicines to people living with the disease. This is what needs to happen in almost every aspect of public life, starting with the 'unwelcome factual truths' of our times. But the telling of truths must be a public act: 'to hide and feel guilty would be the beginning of defeat'. It is this essence of beginning something new that is at the heart of Arendt's conception of what goes on in the public sphere. It is a process of keeping a space open for public deliberation, a space 'where freedom as virtuosity can appear … where freedom is a worldly reality, tangible in words which can be heard, in deeds which can be seen, and in events which are talked about, remembered, and turned into stories before they are finally incorporated into the great storybook of human history.'[28]

What that means of course is that a democratic citizenry is a citizenry with a critical consciousness, for not even the most romantic stories of our past should go unquestioned. Edward Said warns about how every public domain is infested with binary representations of identity, even by former national-ist movements: 'There are great lessons to be learned from decolonisation which are first that, noble as its liberatory aims were, it did not often enough prevent the emergence of repressive nationalist replacements for colonial regimes.' Interestingly, Said argues that the role of intellectuals is to present dispassionate, alternative narratives to those offered by nationalists of all types – both those who were the oppressors and those who, in the name of past suffering, turn around to torment others. One of the challenges we face as we grapple with issues of identity, archive and deliberation is that our inherited notion of archive is one of an inert repository. Said argues that 'our ideas today of archive and discourse must be radically modified' because unlimited audiences and unlimited reproduction through modern technologies have destabilised even the idea of an identifiable audience. 'These things have certainly limited the powers that regimes have to censor or ban writing that is considered dangerous.'[29] This internationalisation of discussions about the archive helps bring other actors to participate in what would have been purely local discussions and turn them into global conversations about the making not only of our nations but of the modern world. This partly explains the international character of the contributions to this book.

THE TRANSMISSION LINES OF THE NEW AFRICAN MOVEMENT

2

NTONGELA MASILELA

The duty of Bantu intellectuals is to create an intellectual awakening which will stimulate thought and set our faculties in motion. This can only be done by organisation, by lectures, debates, reading and writing. Therefore it is important that the educated men of our race should interest themselves in institutions whose aims and objects are the intellectual and spiritual development of the race.[1]

Will our intellectuals be equal to this test? When time comes for constructive thinking and planning will our leaders give a lead on behalf of their people or will they, in turn, be led by the nose by leaders of other races who can be depended upon to seize any opportunity to speak for their followers? Time will show. But we fear that unless our intellectuals get into the sufferings of their people; and weave themselves into their unvoiced fears and anxieties they will never speak the feelings of the people.[2]

THE NEW AFRICAN MOVEMENT AND ITS BEGINNINGS: FROM SOGA TO MQHAYI TO SEME

One fundamental issue encountered in the reconstruction of South African intellectual and cultural history in accordance with the newly emergent epistemic paradigm of the New African Movement is that of establishing a conceptual structure of its periodisation. With whom or with what governing idea should this periodising begin, and how should its end be determined? In his magisterial work *Beginnings*, Edward Said taught generations of postcolonial intellectuals and Third World scholars that the beginnings of intellectual processes are contentious force fields; similarly, in his brilliant book *The Sense of an Ending*, Frank Kermode has postulated the same observations regarding endings.[3]

This was particularly true of the New African Movement, the foundation of which was made necessary by the making and construction of modernity in a context of political domination. Should its beginnings be identified with and demarcated through Pixley ka Isaka Seme who, in 1904, wrote a manifesto, 'The Regeneration of Africa', which unequivocally proclaimed that the beginning of the twentieth century would be the age of modernity in Africa – not only in South Africa – as well as the beginning of the decolonisation process from imperial and colonial domination? Undoubtedly, Seme was responding to, or inspired by, the emergence of two historical forces which were destined to have profound impacts on the modern black world across much of the twentieth century: culturally, New Negro modernity in the United States; and politically, the philosophy of Pan Africanism in the African Diaspora. Pixley ka Isaka Seme was prescient in his historical awareness, since not only did New Negro modernity incubate the Harlem Renaissance in the 1920s (which in turn influenced the formation of the Negritude Movement in Paris in the 1930s, the Haitian Renaissance in Port-au-Prince in the 1930s, and the Sophiatown Renaissance in Johannesburg in the 1950s), but also shaped regulative principles of New African modernity in South Africa. In Anglophone Africa, not only was Pan Africanism recognised as the black philosophy of modernity *par excellence*, it was also acknowledged as a black political ideology which, when combined with emergent African nationalism, accelerated the decolonisation process in the middle of the twentieth century. The political prescience of Seme was such that, nearly sixty years after he unfurled the banner of modernity across Africa, Kwame Nkrumah, the first president of Ghana and arguably the greatest African exponent of Pan Africanism, read the whole of 'The Regeneration of Africa' in his opening address to the First International Congress of Africanists in Accra in 1963, as part of the proceedings.[4]

The beginnings of the New African Movement could equally be associated with the launching of the newspaper *Izwi Labantu* (The Voice of the People) in 1897 by New African intellectuals such as Allan Kirkland, Soga, SEK Mqhayi, Walter Benson Rubusana and Nathaniel Cyril Mhala. The emergence of this intellectual constellation happened at the same time as the formation of the Ethiopian Movement in 1892. Although the Ethiopian Movement constituted the formal founding of Independent African Churches which broke away from the white Christian churches, it was in fact the forging of the incipient form of African nationalism and it signalled the first major ideological struggle against the hegemony of European modernity over the African people. The leading New African intellectual of the *Izwi Labantu* group was SEK Mqhayi who, through the genius of his intellectual and ideological convictions, created and consolidated the cultural 'miracle' of South Africa in the twentieth century: the production of *African literature in the African languages*. Although the New African intellectuals of the golden age of Sotho literature (Thomas Mofolo, Everitt Lechesa Segoete, Zakea D Mangoaela, Azariel M Sekese, Edward Motsamai and Simon Majakatheta Phamotse) preceded Mqhayi in this invention (to be sure, all of them inspired and encouraged by white Christian missionaries), the great Xhosa poet was more historically consequential in begetting several intellectual and cultural traditions of the New African Movement.

First, there came into being formidable scholarship about African languages, initiated by Clement Martyn Doke, followed and supported by exemplary exponents such as AC Jordan, Sophonia Machabe Mofokeng and Benedict Wallet Vilakazi.

Second, in the tracks of Mqhayi's poetic genius expressed in an *African language*, there followed the extraordinary talents of Nontsizi Mgqwetho, Mazisi Kunene, Wallet Benedict Vilakazi, David Livingstone Phakamile Yali-Manisi, KE Ntsane, JJR Jolobe and Stanley Nxu.

Third, by giving legitimacy to the African novel in the African languages with the publication of *Ityala Lama-wele* (The Case of Twins, 1914), Mqhayi made this generic form viable since he was succeeded by Guybon Bundlwana Sinxo, AC Jordan, CLS Nyembezi, BM Khaketla, RRR Dhlomo, TN Maumela, MER Mathivha and Benedict Wallet Vilakazi.

Fourth, in being the greatest exponent of African literature in the African languages, he facilitated a conceptual field in which the history of literature in the African languages would come into being with texts such as DDT Jabavu's *The Influence of English on Bantu Literature* (1921) and *Bantu Literature:Classification and Reviews* (1921), Vilakazi's *The Oral and Written Literature in Nguni* (1946), Mofokeng's *Development of Leading Figures in Animal Tales in Africa* (1954), Jordan's *A Phonological and Grammatical Study of Literary Xhosa* (1956) and *Towards an African Literature* (1973), Kunene's *An Analytical Survey of Zulu Poetry: Both Traditional and Modern* (1959), Nyembezi's *A Review of Zulu Literature* (1961) and Daniel P Kunene's *ThomasMofolo and the Emergence of Written Sesotho Prose* (1980).

Fifth, in writing biographies, and portraits of New Africans in the form of obituaries, Mqhayi initiated a form of intellectual history that was later mastered by HIE Dhlomo, RV Selope Thema, ZK Matthews and Jordan Ngubane. The intellectual history of the New African Movement was arguably best exemplified by TD Mweli Skota's *The African Yearly Register: Being an Illustrated Biographical Dictionary (Who's Who) of Black Folks in Africa* (1930). What is notable about Mweli Skota's undertaking is its transcontinental projection or perspective, and a distinguishing feature of the transmission line made possible by the intellectual and poetic practice of Mqhayi is its *trans-racial* and *trans-ethnic* links. Given this complex achievement, it is as historically plausible to assign the beginnings of the New African Movement to SEK Mqhayi as to Pixley ka Isaka Seme.

On further reflection, however, neither Pixley ka Isaka Seme nor SEK Mqhayi is a historically correct marker for the origins of the New African Movement, for in reality the beginnings of the movement are located at the historical moment of Tiyo Soga (1829-1871), and its trajectory led from Tiyo Soga in the 1860s to Ezekiel Mphahlele (1919-2008) in the 1960s. The historical origins of the New African Movement should be located in Tiyo Soga's philosophical reflections on the necessity of modernity as a result of the catastrophic Nongqawuse episode of 1857 that decimated the Xhosa nation. This episode was the real historical marker between tradition and modernity since it was a consequence of the defeat of African (Xhosa) tradition by European (British) modernity in the Great Frontier Wars of the nineteenth century. It was in these wars that European modernity made its irreversible and violent entrance into African history. In this context, the real importance of Pixley ka Isaka Seme's manifesto of 1904 was perhaps not so much in launching the New African Movement as in being historically conscious that modernity would become the fundamental question for Africa in the twentieth century.

While the Xhosa intellectuals of the 1880s (Elijah Makiwane, John Tengo Jabavu, William Wellington Gqoba, Gwayi Tyamzashe, James Dwane, Pambani Jeremiah Mzimba, Isaac W Wauchope, John Knox Bokwe and Walter Benson Rubusana) had begun to construct a counter-narrative to European modernity in the pages of *Imvo Zabantsundu* (African Opinion) newspaper and through cultural and civic societies such as the Lovedale Literary Society and Native Educational Association, it was Seme's launching of the African National Congress in 1912 that spelled out the necessity of a collective political praxis in transforming European modernity into New African modernity. Mqhayi's cultural practice would not by itself have been enough to effect such a monumental change. From 1912 until the Sharpeville massacre of 1960, the New African Movement and the African National Congress were inseparable, united by a singular historical vision. It was Pixley ka Isaka Seme again in the 1930s, in the pages of *Umteteli wa Bantu*, who began forging the rudimentary forms of African nationalism as an ideological force field that would hold together – in synchrony and in reciprocity with each other – the cultural (the New African Movement) and the political (the African National Congress) wings of New African modernity. With both the African National Congress and African nationalism, Seme established the major transmission line within the New African Movement between the generation of RV Selope Thema (1920s) and that of Jordan Kush Ngubane (1940s and 1950s).

But there are several reasons for according to Tiyo Soga the historical honour of marking the emergence of the New African Movement. First, being the first African to receive the best education European modernity could provide at the time, and consequently being in a real sense the first modern African intellectual, Soga was instantly aware that, with the publication of the first issue of the missionary newspaper *Indaba* in August 1862, newspapers would not only be the forums through which Africans could integrate modern knowledge and traditional knowledge, forming a dialectical synthesis in understanding the ever-changing present – they could also be political instruments for forging a collective African national identity to 'overcome' oppression, backwardness, superstition, animism and licentiousness. He imparted two lessons to the Xhosa intellectuals of the 1880s, many of whom had been his students in their younger days: a belief in the power of newspapers to nurture historical consciousness and change cultural sensibility; and the conviction that religion, preferably Christianity, must be at the centre of such a historical project.

NEWSPAPERS AND PUBLIC INTELLECTUALS

From the founding of the first independent African newspaper *Imvo Zabantsundu* in 1884 by Xhosa intellectuals of the 1880s, to the launching of another independent newspaper *Inkundla ya Bantu* in 1938 by the Zulu intellectual grouping of the 1940s, New African newspapers were both transmission forums of the belief in progress and modernity and vehicles for searching for a plausible process for establishing African unity. At the turn of the nineteenth century and at the beginning of the twentieth century, many newspapers were founded which, fully or partially, consciously or unconsciously, supported Soga's theses: *Izwi Labantu* in 1897; Mark S Radebe's *Iphepha lo Hlanga* (The Paper of the Nation) in 1894; and Solomon T Plaatje's *Koranta ea Becoana* (The Bechuana Gazette) in 1901 (later renamed *Tsala ea Batho* (The People's Friend) in 1910). Mahatma Gandhi's *Indian Opinion* and John Langalibalele Dube's *Ilanga lase Natal* (Natal Sun), both first saw the light of day in 1903.

Two instances could be chosen in which a New African newspaper (here meaning an intellectual forum articulating a New African historical vision, not that it was owned specifically by Africans), sought consciously to construct a tradition of the social responsibilities of intellectuals to an emergent nation under oppressive conditions: these were RV Selope Thema and Henry Selby Msimang in *Umteteli wa Bantu* (The Mouthpiece of the People) in the late 1920s and HIE Dhlomo in *Ilanga lase Natal* in the late 1940s and early 1950s. Thema and Msimang were members of the *Umteteli wa Bantu* group which included the young Dhlomo and others: Nontsizi Mgqwetho, Marshall Maxeke, Richard W Msimang, Abner R Mapanya, Charlotte Manye Maxeke, HT Kumalo, W Davies, JB Mgijima, BS Gumede, J Morolong, JL Moorosi, J Peete, CR Nombewu, GG Kattey, H Kalipa and HD Mohau.

Concerning these issues, Henry Selby Msimang wrote the following articles: 'A Message to the Native National Congress'(24 May 1924); 'Bantu Intellectuals' (12 September-19 October 1925); and 'Ideals: The New Congress'(7 June 1930).

RV Selope Thema himself contributed: 'The Intellectuals'(12 September 1925); 'The Task of Bantu Leadership'(23 October 1926); 'The Test of Bantu Leadership'(27 November 1926); 'Intellectuals and the Chiefs'(3 September 1927); 'The Responsibility of Bantu Intellectuals'(9 March 1929); 'Bantu Leadership'(30 March-13 July 1929); 'The Duty of Bantu Intellectuals'(3 August 1929-23 August 1930); 'The African National Congress: Its Achievements and Failures', I, II, III (1424 September and 3 November 1929); 'Bantu Patriotism'

(6 September 1930); and 'The African National Congress' (14 November 1931).

The articles postulate, in different ways, a position that formed the central consensus of the New African Movement: that without the role of missionaries in bringing Christianity and modern education to the African people, simultaneously with the industrialisation of the country, the transformation effected by the contest between tradition and modernity would not have been possible. The early generations of New African intellectuals were very conscious that they were the outcome of the defeat of traditional societies. This explains the profound ambivalence at the centre of their intellectual practice, whether towards the missionaries, the chiefs or traditional societies; the salutation of the missionaries was concurrent with the damnation of the government by hindering Africans from attaining modern education. This appreciation of the role of missionaries was the constant refrain of earlier generations of New African intellectuals from Solomon T Plaatje through RV Selope Thema to HIE Dhlomo. Whereas the first major debate in the history of New African Movement occurred among the Xhosa intellectuals of the 1880s between Elijah Makiwane and Pambani Jeremiah Mzimba (regarding the role of the English language and English literary culture in enabling Africans to make a transition from tradition to modernity, as well as the role of political practice in modernity), arguably the second major debate occurred among intellectuals of the *Umteteli wa Bantu* group between RV Selope Thema and Henry Selby Msimang about the enabling role of Christianity in the context of an emergent African nationalism.

The second item that concerned *Umteteli wa Bantu* intellectuals in these articles was the social responsibility of New African intelligentsia to the African masses. Whereas an earlier generation of New African intellectuals such as John Langalibalele Dube, Solomon T Plaatje and Pixley ka Isaka Seme were conservative modernisers, amenable to the intervention of chiefs in modern politics, later generations – whose numbers included HIE Dhlomo, Simon Majakathetha Phamotse and SM

Bennett Ncwana – were progressive modernisers, uniformly hostile to such an occurrence. Not only did this younger cohort of intellectuals view chiefs as reactionary stooges of the oppressive white government, they also believed that the chiefs had no understanding or knowledge of the complex nature of modernity. RV Selope Thema and H Selby Msimang both argued that it was African patriotism that unified the interests of the intelligentsia and the masses. In their common struggle against the oppressive government, New African intellectuals had not wanted to be treated more favourably than the common people, but had consistently defended the interests of the African people. They also argued that the African National Congress was the political organisation through which the patriotism of the African people could be articulated and expressed. They affirmed that modernity would enable New African intellectuals to defeat antiquarian forms of enslavement which the government wanted to reactivate and enforce, while holding at bay, as much as they could, modern forms of enslavement re-enacted along class lines. It is clear that in articulating these arguments *Umteteli wa Bantu* intellectuals were reactivating a political and philosophical position first broached by Tiyo Soga approximately half a century earlier: that African intellectuals should utilise Christianity to disengage modernity from its rapacious enabler capitalism. This was the fundamental theme that informed Tiyo Soga's historical project and his writings.

RV SELOPE THEMA AND THE NEW AFRICAN MOVEMENT

RV Selope Thema was unremitting in his denunciation of the 'tyranny' of white oppression and the 'European oligarchy of exploitation' which had given rise to moral degradation and social degeneration among African people. This engagement with the Janus-faced nature of European modernity, its complex historical intertwining of democracy and oppression, was dissipating the moral strength of African people. Consequently, the task of New African intellectuals and political leaders was not only to oppose the political oppression of European modernity but also to formulate social policies, through their own civic and political organisations, that would attempt to change – or at least deflect – the social circumstances that were leading to moral degeneracy. Selope Thema argued that for this reason African people ought to embrace Christian civilisation. Elaborating further and reverting to one of the great themes of his writings, he emphasised that since the New Negroes in the United States had been able to forge New Negro modernity and achieve spectacular things within America modernity just a few decades after the end of their enslavement by fully accepting Christianity, so the New Africans would be able to transform European modernity into New African modernity while achieving significant things in the process by totally aligning themselves with Christian civilisation. There was fierce opposition to this from some New African intellectuals, especially from Henry Selby Msimang, a close personal friend and a colleague of Selope Thema within the *Umteteli wa Bantu* intellectual constellation.

These contestations will be considered elsewhere, but here several observations need to be made. First, the echo of Tiyo Soga in Selope Thema's arguments is clear because – arguably – he absorbed the Lovedale (that is, Xhosa) intellectual tradition more profoundly than any New African intellectual. Inspired by the preaching and proselytising of the sixty-year-old Elijah Makiwane among the Pedi people in the hinterlands of the Zoutpansberg in 1902 or 1903, the seventeen-year-old Selope Thema committed himself to modernity and Christianity by later going to study at Lovedale, with Booker T Washington's *Up From Slavery* under his arm. The utmost seriousness with which Selope Thema absorbed the Xhosa/Christian/Lovedale intellectual tradition was to make him one of the strongest transmission lines within the New African Movement.[5] It is not surprising therefore that when he became the founding editor of *The Bantu World* in 1932 he gave ample space to SEK Mqhayi to publish as much as he wanted in its pages, thereby facilitating one of the great poet's most productive periods. It was Selope Thema himself who transmitted the Xhosa intellectual tradition to the young New African intellectuals who worked as his assistants on the newspaper: Peter Segale, HIE Dhlomo, Peter Abrahams, Guybon Bundlwana Sinxo, RRR Dhlomo, Walter MB Nhlapo, Jordan Kush Ngubane, Henry Nxumalo and Todd Matshikiza.

Second, most likely through the Xhosa Intellectuals of the 1880s, Selope Thema familiarised himself more deeply and extensively with New Negro intellectuals such as Frederick Douglass, Booker T Washington and Alexander Crummell. Inasmuch as Crummell had influenced Elijah Makiwane and his cohorts on the passageways from African tradition to European modernity, so he indicated to Selope Thema and his generation of New African intellectuals the possible bridgeheads from European modernity to New African modernity. In the pages of *The Bantu World* Selope Thema transmitted both the Xhosa intellectual tradition and the New Negro intellectual tradition. But he and other conservative modernisers made a major shift: to rate Booker T Washington as more important than Alexander Crummell for New African historical imperatives. Other New African intellectuals disagreed, and rightfully designated WEB Du Bois as the central intellectual of New Negro modernity.

Third, the choice of Booker T Washington as his 'master' located RRV Selope Thema among the conservative modernisers, when in reality he would have wanted posterity to see him as among the progressive modernisers. His conservatism was very much apparent to later generations of New African intellectuals of the Sophiatown Renaissance (Henry Nxumalo, 'The Most Controversial Man in Black Politics,' *Drum*, April 1953; Matthew Nkoana, 'The Man Who Fought For Better Race Relations,' *Golden City Post*, 18 September 1955). It was in this camp that he fought in the 1930s to defeat the revolutionary modernisers (Albert Nzula, James La Guma, Josiah Tshangana Gumede, Edwin Mofutsanyana, Johannes Nkosi, John Gomas, Moses M Kotane and IB Tabata) within the New African Movement when the struggle between Marxism and African nationalism ensued. Thema had a tonic effect on the Zulu intellectuals of the 1940s such as Anton Lembede and Jordan Kush Ngubane in their defence of African nationalism within the African National Congress in later decades. Inasmuch as Elijah Makiwane (a Xhosa) intellectually transformed RV Selope Thema (a Pedi), so Selope Thema himself did the same to Jordan Kush Ngubane (a Zulu). This makes clear that the transaction of influences across the splay of the New African Movement was across ethnic lines, and it twisted those lines in uncharacteristic ways. The convergence of the political philosophy of conservative modernisers such as Pixley ka Isaka Seme and RV Selope Thema was what made Jordan Kush Ngubane so troublesome and so formidable in the 1950s, particularly in his contentious quarrels with the revolutionary modernisers FT Mofutsanyana, Yusuf Dadoo and Ruth First, and the progressive modernisers Albert Luthuli, Nelson Mandela (respectively, 'S. A. P. Commentary', *Inkundla ya Bantu*, 29 February 1944; 'Smear Tactics Again: Some Queries', *Indian Opinion*, 4 September 1953; 'From The Sidelines', *Fighting Talk*, August 1956: 'A Reply To Mr Jordan K Ngubane's 'Attacks: On The African National Congress', *Indian Opinion*, 27 June-6 July 1956; 'Towards Democratic Unity', *Liberation*, No. 6, November 1953). When a definitive history of the New African Movement is written it may turn out that the conservative modernisers were intellectually more formidable and politically more sophisticated in practice than the progressive and the revolutionary modernisers. It was not so much the defeat of socialism by capitalism in 1989 that led the African National Congress post-1994 to reconcile itself with conservatism as much as the remarkable resilience of the intellectual force of conservative modernisers in the history of the New African Movement.

The writings of RV Selope Thema and Henry Selby Msimang indicate that perhaps the first major intellectual consideration of the role of New African political leadership within the African National Congress occurred in the late 1920s and early 1930s. This political entanglement among conservative modernisers was between Thema and Msimang on the one hand, and Seme (then secretary general of the African National Congress) on the other. Selope Thema outlined the fundamental social responsibility of New African political leadership as the fostering of African unity in the struggle for freedom in opposition to provincialism, tribalism and white domination. It was the struggle against the Hertzog Bills in the 1920s and 1930s that galvanised the New African political leadership. Selope Thema spelled out their consequences: abolition of the African voting franchise in the Cape Province; entrenchment of the policy of racial segregation; enhancement of the position of the chiefs against the leadership of New African intellectuals by strengthening of the tribal system. Not only would the progress of African people towards modernity be halted, but they would be reduced to serfdom; the seeds of the destruction of African unity would be sown. The conservatism of Selope Thema was apparent in the distinction he made: his opposition to white exploitation, oppression and tyranny did not mean he wanted to overthrow white rule; it was based on a *moral* critique of capitalism rather than the *class* critique promulgated by revolutionary modernisers.

Not confining his criticism to white leadership, Selope Thema also criticised the organisational structure of the African National Congress and the leadership skills of Pixley ka Isaka Seme. He thought that the constitution of the national organisation was in disharmony with that of the provinces. In consequence, the political leadership of the provinces challenged the constitutionality and authority of the national leadership and, given this disharmony, he felt that the New African political leadership would not be able effectively to defend the New African masses against white oppression. Selope Thema argued that the political leadership of Seme was dictatorial rather than democratic as it was based on the absence of policy and programme and a disdain for collective consultation. Henry Selby Msimang also saw dictatorship in this leadership since Seme saw himself as embodying the organisation rather than serving the interests of the African people by means of the organisation.

Seme responded to these criticisms by defining his historical vision of the African National Congress ('The African National Congress', *Umteteli wa Bantu*, 26 November 1932; 'The African National Congress', *Umteteli wa Bantu*, 10 December 1932; 'The Nation's Call', *Umteteli wa Bantu*, 31 December 1932). The criticisms of Seme by Thema and Msimang were endorsed by most members of the New African intelligentsia and Seme was unceremoniously but democratically removed from the leadership of the African National Congress within a few years of these astringent critiques.

THE CULTURAL MODERNITY OF HIE DHLOMO

HIE Dhlomo had worked with RV Selope Thema and Henry Selby Msimang as colleagues in the *Umteteli wa Bantu* intellectual group of the 1920s, and for a short time under the editorial leadership of Thema in *The Bantu World* in the 1930s. It is therefore is not surprising that in the 1940s, as deputy editor of *Ilanga lase Natal*, Dhlomo engaged with the role of New African intellectuals and the nature of New African political leadership with much greater depth than his senior colleagues. From these two preceding intellectual constellations of the New African Movement, Dhlomo brought the role of intellectuals to the centre of cultural preoccupations of the Zulu intellectuals of the 1940s (Benedict Wallet Vilakazi, Nimrod Njabulo Ndebele, DGS Mtimkulu, Rueben Caluza, CLS Nyembezi, Walter MB Nhlapo, Mazisi Kunene, Albert Luthuli, Jacob M Nhlapo, Anton Lembede, Jordan Kush Ngubane, Emman AM Made, Gerald Bhengu, RRR Dhlomo, Kenneth Bhengu and JJC Dlamini). Like Thema, Dhlomo paid homage to the modern Xhosa intellectual tradition ('An Impression', *Umteteli wa Bantu*, 12 July 1930). In fact, he was the principal conduit of this tradition to the Zulu intellectuals of the 1940s. It was therefore not surprising that it was the members of this constellation (HIE Dhlomo, Jordan Kush Ngubane and Walter MMB Nhlapo) who wrote some of the most memorable words on the occasion of the passing away of SEK Mqhayi in 1945.

Among the first things Dhlomo did concerning the social responsibility of intellectuals was to give historical resonance and sociological density to the construct of 'New African' in the 1940s. Since its invention by Thema during the 1920s in the pages of *Umteteli wa Bantu*, the concept had been largely a periodising marker between the historical moment of New Africans and that of chiefs. In fact, immediately after he invented this construct it practically disappears from Thema's discourse for the remaining decades of his intellectual practice. Solomon T Plaatje also intervened in these matters, preferring to speak of the 'New Native' rather than the 'New African'; viewing the New Native from the perspective of tradition, Plaatje was critical of the New Africans, judging them to be full of the spirit of lawlessness and egoism, incapable of distinguishing between good and bad, having no moral depth – which was evident in the disbelief of tradition and custom ('The New Native and the New Year', *Umteteli wa Bantu*, 12 January 1929; 'The Good New Times' and the 'New Native', *Umteteli wa Bantu*, 9 November 1929). Although from the moment of the invention of the concept of the 'New African' there have been both positive and negative evaluations, Selope Thema's perspective, oriented towards the future, has prevailed over that of Plaatje which was governed by the weight of the past. Dhlomo inherited the positive construct of the New African intellectual.

After he had recalled and appropriated this construct, HIE Dhlomo's intellectual work changed dramatically, shifting from a preoccupation with culture to cultural politics and finally to politics, a political awareness informed by internationalism and cosmopolitanism. The marker of this monumental shift was the great prose poems that HIE Dhlomo wrote in the late 1940s in the pages of *Ilanga lase Natal*. Although Dhlomo had earlier begun writing in earnest about intellectuals, in two pieces ('Our Intellectuals', *Ilanga lase Natal*, 31 July 1943 and 'Intellectuals and Congress, *Ilanga lase Natal*, 2 November 1946), following on his recollection of the construct of the New African ('Racial Attitudes: An African Viewpoint', *The Democrat*, 17 November 1945 and 'African Attitudes', *The Democrat*,

1 December 1945), it was in his editorial 'Problems of African Leadership' in *Ilanga lase Natal* (12 February 1948) that he systematically engaged the phenomenon of New African intellectuals as pathfinders or enlighteners towards modernity.

Articulating a longitudinal perspective in 'Problems of African Leadership', Dhlomo situates the formation of New African intellectuals and political leadership in the context of South African political and social history. He argues that the industrialisation and urbanisation of the country during the First World War (1914-1918) and the Second World War (1939-1945), and oppressive political acts such as the Native Land Act of 1913 and the Hertzog Bills of 1936, had several transformative effects on African people. First, their historical consciousness changed from tribal allegiances to national alliances. Second, they began to think of leadership in collective terms rather than as a matter of personalities. Third, the emergence of the African middle class and the African working class necessitated establishing political leadership across class lines. It was these changes that made possible the formation of the African National Congress in 1912 and the Industrial and Commercial Workers' Union in 1919. The launching of the political organisation and the labour union was part of the construction of the counter-narrative of New African modernity against the imperatives and edicts of European modernity. Dhlomo is explicit in identifying New Africanness with democratic collective leadership in opposition to the dictatorial tribal 'great leadership' of the chiefs. The New African leadership was based on principles and policies rather than on the personalities and individualism that characterised the leadership of the chiefs. For Dhlomo, the struggle between the New African intellectuals (political leadership) and the African chiefs was the fundamental historical dividing line between tradition and modernity.

The consciousness of this historical divide explains his unremitting hostility toward the chiefs. A nuanced contrast between Dhlomo and Selope Thema needs to be indicated: Dhlomo's hatred for the chiefs was because he felt they were a hindrance to the progressive transformation of tradition in accordance with the imperatives of New African modernity which was labouring under the oppressive conditions of European modernity; Selope Thema was unshakeable in his belief that New African modernity could only succeed on the basis of the destruction of tradition. Because he was constantly searching for a creative process to overcome this intractable triadic struggle (African tradition, European modernity, and New African modernity), Dhlomo was to reflect longer and in much greater depth than any other New African on the nature and social responsibilities of New African intellectuals and political leadership. The aforementioned articles were part of a historical, social, political and cultural search for the praxis and process by which New African modernity could overcome and transform European modernity. Dhlomo is explicit in indicating that it was the *new politics* of the African National Congress Youth League in the 1940s that was an inspiration to his searches for New African intellectualism.

HIE Dhlomo sketched several short intellectual portraits of New Africans in *Ilanga lase Natal* while seeking to delineate the nature of New African intellectual culture: 'Snaps: RT Caluza', 24 May 1947; 'Snaps: DGS Mtimkhulu', 14 June 1947; 'Snaps: WJ Mseleku', 9 August 1947; 'Snaps: Dr BW Vilakazi', 16 August 1947; 'Snaps: Gerald Bhengu', 23 August 1947; 'Snaps: Mrs AJ Sililo', 30 August 1947; 'Snaps: KE Masinga', 13 September 1947; 'Snaps: Miss Bertha Mkize', 20 September 1947; 'Weekly Letter: To Chief AJ Luthuli', 1 April 1950; 'Weekly Letter: To Edward Jali', 8 April 1950; 'Weekly Letter: To EHA Made', 22 April 1950; 'Weekly Letter: To H Selby Msimang', 29 April 1950; 'Weekly Letter: JD Nyaose', 27 May 1950; 'Weekly Letter: RT Caluza', 3 June 1950. In each of these portraits Dhlomo was singularly concerned to indicate that modern education was fundamentally important to their distinctive achievements of defining and articulating a 'New African'. What really engaged him was not so much the nature of the education in and of itself as much as the intellectual and artistic realisations that expressed the New African historical experience of modernity. Having had an excellent education at Ohlange Institute (founded by John Langalibalele Dube in the early years of the twentieth century), and at the historically black American university, Hampton Institute, Dhlomo marvelled at how this had enabled Reuben Caluza to compose outstanding string quartet pieces while doing impressive research on indigenous music. Dhlomo found Caluza exemplary in having entered the profession of pedagogics and becoming the Principal of Adams College School of Music. Concerning DGS Mtimkulu, Dhlomo emphasised the three MA degrees he had obtained at Fort Hare, Yale University and the University of London which enabled him to take leadership roles in various civic, social and cultural organisations: principal of Ohlange Institute; president of the Natal Teachers' Union; president of the South African Teachers' Federation; executive member of the Institute of Race Relations; chairman of the local branch of the Christian Council; and member of the Natal African Education Advisory Board. At the same time as these civic responsibilities, Mtimkulu was a passionate sports participant.

Dhlomo praised Gerald Bhengu, who lacked formal education, for having educated himself and becoming one of the best New African painters, and he pointed out that, in addition to painting, Bhengu illustrated school books (he spent many years teaching at Nuttall College in Edendale). Dhlomo praised KE Masinga as a newspaper columnist of high ethical standards as well as a popular radio broadcaster of his own plays and those of young and talented African playwrights. Besides being a leading radio dramatist, he also conducted choirs with which he travelled as far as present day Zambia, Zimbabwe, Angola and Mozambique. Dhlomo singled out Bertha Mkhize for having been at the 'forefront of the struggles for National Liberation' and for being a leading member of various prominent organisations such as the Daughters of Africa, African National Congress, and the Industrial and Commercial Workers' Union.

This selective reading of the vast repertoire of intellectual portraits that HIE Dhlomo sketched over a decade in *Ilanga lase Natal* shows his own particular understanding of the nature of the New African intellectual, beyond the conceptual space invented by RV Selope Thema.

First, Dhlomo gave greater amplitude to the idea of the New African intellectual by making it inclusive of females. This was certainly beyond what a conservative moderniser like Selope Thema had in mind. Dhlomo's predecessor in this inclusiveness of the New African intellectual was SEK Mqhayi in the pages of *Imvo Zabantsundu* in the 1920s and those of *Umteteli wa Bantu* in the 1930s. Mqhayi poetically memorialised women intellectual and political leaders such as Charlotte Manye Maxeke and Mina Soga, the granddaughter of Tiyo Soga. In the pages of the *Golden City Post* in the 1950s, Ezekiel Mphahlele continued the tradition of Mqhayi and Dhlomo by celebrating Helen Joseph and Lilian Ngoyi as exemplary intellectuals and political leaders.

Second, although Dhlomo saw himself as a classical intellectual in the sense of being principally occupied with writerly matters, and emotively attached to hegemonic cultural expressive forms like classical music, he was hostile to jazz. He shared this attitude with practically all the New African intellectuals (the only exception being Walter MB Nhlapo). Until the emergence of the Sophiatown Renaissance intellectuals of the 1950s, he seems to have instinctively felt that 'the popular' and 'the classical' in New African intellectualism should not be antagonistically separate from each other as in European modernity in South Africa. Dhlomo seems to have attained this historical consciousness in the 1930s when he was struggling to mingle indigenous traditional drama and European drama in order to arrive at New African theatre. This was the decade of his historical dramas as well as the extraordinary formulations of the literary theory of New African drama – in effect a social theory of the historical divide between modernity and tradition. This was the time when Dhlomo also spoke of himself as participating in the 'African Drama Movement'.

Third, in his estimation, New African intellectuals should be as much about the *transmission of knowledge* as about the *production of knowledge*. This may partly be explained by the fact that he was as much attuned to the *voice* as he was to the *printed word*, as is evident from his dramas, voluminous poetry and passion for music recitals. It was not accidental that HIE Dhlomo and Mark S Radebe, the first serious New African music critic in the pages of *Umteteli wa Bantu* in the 1930s, were the founders of the Eisteddfod music competitions in the Transvaal.[6]

DHLOMO ON BW VILAKAZI

Despite his somewhat ambivalent attitude towards canonical intellectual distinctions, HIE Dhlomo was enamoured of Benedict Wallet Vilakazi, one of the most classical of all New African intellectuals, who was unapologetic about his canonising ways. In an essay on the Zulu poet EAH Made, Dhlomo made an observation that makes comprehensible why he was preoccupied with New African intellectual culture, especially in the last decade of his life: he observed that the true greatness of a people depends upon its creative and inventive genius – philosophers, poets, painters, writers, musicians and creative scientists ('Emman AH Made: An Appreciation', *Ilanga lase Natal*, 6 November 1948). In passing, he bracketed Vilakazi with the 'Xhosa creative spirits' SEK Mqhayi, JJR Jolobe, AC Jordan and John Knox Bokwe. In the aforementioned 'Weekly Letter to EHA Made', in a series with the other aforementioned intellectual portraits, Dhlomo wrote the following:

> Conditions in South Africa are such that the African Race lives as a Nation engaged in a terrible and decisive war. Our manhood is degraded daily. Our children starve, cry and die. Our country is not our own. In times such as these a Race must mobilize and marshal all its forces. And one of these forces are words. It is the writer's duty and privilege to wield this mighty weapon successfully or unsuccessfully for the sake of the Cause and his country: of his compatriots, children, his, our, humanity ... We as a people

are engaged in a war of liberation, self-determination and self-expression. It is a titanic struggle of ideas at war, the clash of cultures, the lowering of values, the confusion of issues, and the deliberate and subtle obscuring of ideologies and fundamentals. It is a supreme battle against Truth and natural law. The writer's duty is to give ammunition and inspiration to our defenders, fighters; ideas and expression to the illiterate and inarticulate; balm and hope to the oppressed, the despairing and [the] lowliest. He must mirror and tell of the people, reveal their soul and suffering, expose their exploitation, fight by their side, sing their tribulations and triumphs, their naked practical experiences and their hidden, flaming and unconquerable spiritual valour ... To do this, the writer must identify himself with his people. He must exploit, bleed and give of himself. That is were great creative souls in art, science and literature transcend mere politicians, opportunists and others. They do not use events or people and their weakness and troubles to climb to power and popularity but have to crucify and dig painfully into themselves in order to serve and give to the people. This is your task and that of your fellow writers. Africa demands it of you. We do not seek or wait your reply. *We conscript you to duty* [my emphasis].

These are among the most extraordinary words HIE Dhlomo wrote in three decades (1924 to 1954) of intellectual activity within New African modernity. In conscripting Made, Dhlomo was also conscripting all other New African intellectuals. This 'Weekly Letter to EHA Made' should be viewed as one of the manifestos of the New African Movement, very much in line with Seme's founding manifesto 'The Regeneration of Africa'.

The poems of Nontsizi Mgqwetho, particularly those that appeared in the spectacular year of 1924 in *Umteteli wa Bantu*, deserve also to be given this recognition. One could also include here the remarkable words of Clement Martyn Doke, a philosophical credo emphasising the centrality of African languages in the then emergent modern African culture ('A

Call to Philological Study and Research in South Africa', *The South African Quarterly*, July 1925/February 1926). That Benedict Wallet Vilakazi exemplified this philosophical credo in his poetic activity, creative process and scholarly endeavours is evident in his constant presence in the intellectual imagination of Dhlomo from 1938 ('The Conception and Development of Poetry in Zulu,' *Ilanga lase Natal*, 20 August) to 1952 ('Dr Vilakazi', *Drum*, July), the latter written five years after the death of the great poet at the age of 41 in 1947. Both Made and Dhlomo were shattered by the passing of Vilakazi, as were many other New African intellectuals. Made wrote an elegy in isiZulu immediately after Vilakazi died which was translated into English by Dhlomo (the only translation he is known to have done).[7]

There can be no doubt that Dhlomo viewed Vilakazi as the most classical of the New African intellectuals within the New African Movement, which does not necessarily mean that he was the most original – he was the most classical because of the organic nature of his interdisciplinary *oeuvre* (scholar, poet, novelist, essayist) and because he embodied the most impressive ethical principles in commitment to serious intellectual work. One of the things Dhlomo admired most about Vilakazi was his utmost commitment to education as a lifelong process: upon completing his Doctorate of Literature (D Litt) at the University of Witwatersrand in 1946, a year before his death, Vilakazi contemplated going either to Cambridge University or Oxford University to pursue a 'further degree' of Doctor of Philosophy in Literature, in order to study among the best minds in the world. This quest or search for the world's best in education was congruent with the enormity of his ambition, which Dhlomo characterised as threefold in the *Drum* article: a) to be so productive in intellectual work that his time would be recognised by posterity as the 'Vilakazi Age in African Studies'; b) to be acknowledged as a leading world intellectual on African cultural matters on the basis of scholarly work he had hoped to start immediately upon completing his ambitious education – his collaboration with Clement Martyn Doke on the great *Zulu-English Dictionary* was perhaps a foretaste of what he intended to achieve by himself; c) to impose his scholarly authority on European scholars wherever they were to be found, in all corners of the world, on matters concerning Africa. Dhlomo observes that it was the combination of his enormous ambition and extraordinary intellect that made a contingent of New African intellectuals bestow on him the sobriquet of the 'Cultural Bambatha of the African People'. Dhlomo never doubted that had Vilakazi not died so relatively young he would have been able to fulfill his remarkable ambitions. Among the things that impressed Dhlomo most about Vilakazi were the practical steps he took towards establishing an African Academy of Arts and Research, an idea that had been proposed by Doke a decade earlier (HIE Dhlomo, 'Academy of Arts and Research', *Ilanga lase Natal*, 10 September 1949). The actualisation of this idea unfortunately died with Vilakazi.

Although Dhlomo was dazzled by Vilakazi's virtuosity in fiction, poetry and scholarship, he did not believe Vilakazi excelled in each of them with equal force. After reviewing one of his novels upon its publication ('*U-Dingiswayo ka Jobe*: An Appreciation', *Ilanga lase Natal*, 14 December 1940), he never again mentioned Vilakazi as a novelist. He tabulated several defects that prevented Vilakazi from being an excellent novelist: the tendency towards moralising that distracts from the literary and artistic value of the work; the standoffish manner regarding his characters which constantly results in their being criticised as though they were real human beings; and the absence of emotional complexity in the characters, who tend to reside on the surface of things. With this 'appreciation' Dhlomo bade farewell to Vilakazi as a novelist and the subsequent articles he wrote on Vilakazi were invariably about his poetry and his breakthrough scholarship. Fifteen years later, in the *Drum* appraisal, Dhlomo does not even mention that Vilakazi had written three novels in isiZulu. In this last article he was to write about his great friend, just four years before his own death, he predicted that in all probability posterity would remember Benedict Wallet Vilakazi for having been a seminal scholar. Indeed, posterity (in the form of AC Jordan, Mazisi Kunene and Daniel Kunene) has bestowed high esteem on Vilakazi's doctoral dissertation, 'Oral And Written Literature in Nguni', because of its originality and as the first major literary history of African literature in the African languages.

THE POLITICAL MODERNITY OF RUBUSANA, JABAVU AND ZK MATTHEWS

Vilakazi's doctoral dissertation indicates a strong affinity for modern Xhosa intellectual culture (he writes that the first three decades of South African cultural history should be designated as 'The Age of Walter Benson Rubusana'), particularly as it was represented by SEK Mqhayi, the greatest exponent of African literature in the African languages in the New African Movement. Indeed, Vilakazi was so strongly aligned with Mqhayi that he did not hesitate to launch into a historic duel with Dhlomo in 1938 for writing his historical drama as well as his poetry in English rather than in an African language. Nonetheless, the intellectual relationship between Vilakazi and Dhlomo is the most fascinating in the constellation of the Zulu intellectuals of the 1940s, surpassing that between Vilakazi and Jordan Ngubane or between Dhlomo and Jordan Ngubane. Dhlomo's one fundamental criticism of Vilakazi was his apolitical nature, which he would have characterised as that of a conservative moderniser, since Vilakazi was closer to conservative political leaders like John Langalibalele Dube and AWG Champion despite his apathy towards politics.

There were two other New African intellectuals Dhlomo admired for their intellectual acumen, rather than for their political skills or their creative talent *per se*: DDT Jabavu and ZK Matthews. On the occasion of Jabavu's retirement as Professor of Bantu (African) Languages at Fort Hare, Dhlomo paid tribute to him as a fine writer and journalist, who had written several books, and served the African people politically as president of the All African Convention ('Prof DDT Jabavu,' *Ilanga lase*

Natal, 4 November 1944). No doubt Dhlomo situated him in the canonical membership of the New African Movement ('Great Pioneers of the Movement,' *Ilanga lase Natal*, 30 June 1951; 'The Peacock of Somtseu Barracks,' *Ilanga laseNatal*, 15 August 1953). Dhlomo also regarded Matthews as a great pioneer of the Movement to whom he devoted a whole editorial page celebrating the quality of his critical thinking ('The Next 25 Years', *Ilanga lase Natal*, 2 October 1948). He also paid tribute to Matthews for having suggested the idea of calling a convention of African people, a suggestion that eventually led to the Congress of the People of 1955 that drafted the Freedom Charter of the African National Congress ('The Problems of the African National Congress,' *Ilanga lase Natal*, 17 October 1953). What was characteristic of Jabavu and Matthews in this context was their membership of what I would characterise as the 'Xhosa aristocracy' of the Xhosa intellectual tradition: the former by birth as a son of John Tengo Jabavu, founder of the *Imvo Zabantsundu* newspaper in 1884 who was also a member of the Xhosa intellectual grouping of the 1880s; the latter by marrying Frieda Bokwe, daughter of the biographer of Ntsikana (the first Xhosa convert into Christianity), John Knox Bokwe, who was also a member of the Xhosa intellectuals of the 1880s. One had to have gone to Lovedale to expect inclusion in the aristocracy. Education and intelligence were necessary prerequisites to membership: DDT Jabavu by being the first African to receive a BA degree from an English university in the humanities rather than in theology as had Tiyo Soga, approximately thirty years earlier; Matthews for having been one of the first two Africans to graduate from Fort Hare a few years after its founding in 1916. In her autobiography *Remembrances* (1995), Frieda Bokwe Matthews tells of how Matthews, a Tswana, faced constant interrogation from her uncles, when he expressed his desire to marry their niece, for having an English rather than an African name – what made matters worse is that while her father was very much for the marriage, her brother Roseberry Bokwe (who was also Matthews's best friend at Fort Hare) strangely enough was hostile to the prospect of his sister marrying an 'outsider'. The wisdom of Xhosa elders won the day against the petulance of an up and coming brilliant New African intellectual. Subsequent to this fascinating episode, Roseberry obtained a medical degree from Scotland, and Matthews received an MA degree from Yale University. Matthews's MA thesis, *Bantu Law and Western Civilisation in South Africa: A Study in the Clash of Cultures* (1934), is one of the foremost documents of the New African Movement. It is also a classic case study of how European modernity in South Africa was subverted from within into New African modernity.

The primary importance of ZK Matthews here is that, like RV Selope Thema, he was one of the fundamental transmission lines of Xhosa intellectual tradition throughout the splay of the New African Movement. His 1925 appointment as principal of Adams College in Natal, where Albert Luthuli was his colleague, and Anton Lembede and Jordan Ngubane his students, enabled him to transmit this intellectual tradition to the Zulu nation as it was seriously engaged with the meaning of modernity. Both Lembede and Ngubane were in later years members of the Zulu intellectuals of the 1940s (including also Luthuli) and founding members of the African National Congress Youth League in 1944. An extended and thorough appraisal of the intellectual and political legacy of Matthews by Jordan Ngubane, approximately twenty years after their first encounter, paid tribute to his intellectual brilliance and the effect he had had on those of his students who were now his formidable colleagues ('African Viewpoint: Prof ZK Matthews', *Indian Opinion*, 26 June 1953). What made the Zulu intellectuals of the 1940s the most formidable constellation in the history of the New African Movement was the synthesis of three different intellectual traditions: the Xhosa intellectual tradition of SEK Mqhayi; the modern English intellectual tradition of Shakespeare; and the indigenous Zulu intellectual tradition of Magolwane, Mshongweni and Lydia Umkasetemba, stemming from the militarism of Shaka.

HIE Dhlomo and Benedict Wallet Vilakazi were the most outstanding synthesisers of this triadic structure. The intellectual, artistic and political brilliance of the Zulu intellectuals of the 1940s explains their having been in the forefront of transforming European modernity into New African modernity. ZK Matthews was as responsible as any other 'outsider' for shaping its intellectual armour.

The immediate concern of ZK Matthews to us here is that, like RS Selope Thema, Henry Selby Msimang and HIE Dhlomo, he wrote quite extensively on the role of New African intellectuals in the history of the Movement. Since his catalogue was written a year after the defeat of the New African Movement by the apartheid state at the time of the Sharpeville massacre in 1960, his retrospective appraisals had the effect of a valedictory recollection of a political and cultural movement that had done so much in the construction of modernity but had been unexpectedly and violently terminated. This last snapshot of the New African intellectuals positioned the Xhosa intellectual tradition at the centre of the New African movement. It appeared in *ImvoZabantsundu* from 3 June to 21 November 1961. The portraits are impressive for their wide ranging nature: John Tengo Jabavu (10 June), Davidson Don Tengo Jabavu (17 June), Solomon T Plaatje (24 June and 1 July), Pambani Jeremiah Mzimba (8 July), Noni Jabavu (15 July), John L Dube (22 July), John Knox Bokwe (29 July and 5 August), RV Selope Thema (12 August), Meschach Pelem (19 August), Walter B Rubusana (26 August), Thomas M Mapikela (2 September), Charlotte Manye Maxeke (9 September), 'Prof' James Thaele (16 September), Isaiah Bud-Mbelle (23 September), Hamilton Masiza (30 September), Paul Xiniwe (7 October), SEK Mqhayi (14 October), Elijah Makiwane (21 October), SM Makgatho (28 October), Charles Dube (4 November), William Samuel Mazwi (11 November), Alfred Mangena (18 November) and Pixley ka Isaka Seme (21 November). Although AB Xuma was not included in this galaxy of New African intellectuals, his death a few months after it had been concluded inspired ZK Matthews to write a tribute to his contributions to the making of New

African political modernity ('Tribute to late Dr AB Xuma', *Imvo Zabantsundu*, 10 February 1962).

In a prolegomenon to the series ('Our Heritage', 3 June), ZK Matthews stated the reasons why the legacy of the New African intellectuals' struggle to construct modernity should not be forgotten by future generations:

> In this series of articles I propose to deal with the lives and times of African men and women who have played or are playing a significant part in the development of their people. It would of course be impossible to examine even in a limited way all of them or to deal fully with any of them. The number of people who contribute to the progress of a people in various aspects of their life is in the nature of things very great. Some make their contribution in places or in careers or in ways which bring them into the limelight, so that their fellows readily recognise their gifts ... We must place on record for the benefit of our readers, especially the rising generation, something of the rich heritage or endeavour by their forefathers which they might emulate or from which they might draw inspiration ... I believe it is difficult if not impossible to inspire people who know little or nothing of what was gone on before them. Such people are apt to imagine that everything in the world started when they were born and will end when they pass out of existence ... Because our world is very largely a man-made-world, there is undoubtedly a tendency for us to underestimate or minimise the part which women can play of have played in our national development.

All the portraits of New African intellectuals written during the New African movement, from Pixley ka Isaka Seme on Alfred Mangena ('Alfred Mangena of Lincoln's Inn: Esquire and Barrister-at-Law', *Ilanga laseNatal*, 14 August 1908) to Lewis Nkosi on Robert Sobukwe ('Robert Sobukwe: An Assessment', *Africa Report*, April 1962), were guided by this historical principle.

In post-apartheid South Africa a simple historical fact confronts us: the *idea* of an African renaissance is unrealisable without the knowledge of the *history* of the New African movement which led from the moment of Tiyo Soga to the moment of Ezekiel Mphahlele.

SOME DO CONTEST THE ASSERTION THAT I AM AN AFRICAN

3

FREDERIK VAN ZYL SLABBERT

A few introductory remarks about my own philosophical development will help to contextualise the issue that I want to focus on. The issue is on the one hand an invented historiography – the invention of history – and the harm it does to a society; and then, on the other hand, the use of race as an instrument of policy implementation.

I must say at the outset that for me the concept 'race' has no scientific basis whatsoever, but the fact that people believe it makes it real in its consequences; and it is those consequences that we have to deal with most of the time.

The Nationalist Party came to power in 1948. I was at that time in Standard One at Jan Cilliers Laerskool here in Parkview. My classmates were Hendrik Verwoerd, Nico Diederichs and MC Botha – obviously, the sons of the fathers of the Nationalist Party.

After Standard One I was whisked away with my twin sister to Marabastad farm school, 17 miles this side of Polokwane (it's no longer called Marabastad, I think it's called Eerstegoud). There, for the very first time, I really saw and experienced the tail end of Afrikaner poor white-ism. Those were seriously, seriously poor people, and although my grandfather could afford shoes for me, the idea was that we would not wear shoes so as not to shame those who could not afford them, so we all walked around barefoot, winter and summer, and I felt at the end of the winter that I could dropkick a brick from the quarter-line over the poles.

I went to Pietersburg High School and for various reasons became born-again and decided I wanted to become a *dominee* (a priest). I went to Wits University for my first year because there I could do classical studies such as Greek and Latin but they didn't have classical Hebrew. In my first year, the Pan Africanist Congress leader Robert Sobukwe was teaching African languages. I remember going to one of his lectures, and it was absolutely packed. In fact I felt a bit like Piet Retief there. There were hardly any whites in that audience. Robert Sobukwe gave his talk and a timid Indian student got up, and said, 'Do you really think you people are ready to govern?' And, like one person, the audience jumped out of their chairs and screamed, 'Right now!' Now, for me coming from Pietersburg, this was the most exotic idea I had ever heard of in my life. I could not believe it.

That was one formative experience. Another profound impact on me centered on Professor Eddie Roux, who was head of the Rationalist Thinkers Forum or Rationalist Society. Someone from the Fellowship Society gave a lecture 'Did Christ Rise from the Dead?' which I attended. A week later, Eddie Roux advertised his lecture saying, 'Did Cinderella Lose her Glass Slipper?', 'Did Jack Really Climb the Beanstalk?' Now, for me, this was blasphemous in the extreme.

In any case, I went to Stellenbosch for my second year because they had classical Hebrew there. I did missionary work in the townships but in the meantime, of course, Sharpeville happened. And just to show you how politically oblivious I was, I went with a professor of missionary science to go and do missionary work in Langa just after Sharpeville. We were suddenly surrounded by a group of very, very angry people. They started throwing stones at us and they marched us out. I looked up the street and there was the professor of missionary science, a dear old man (we called him Oom Klaasvakie because he always fell asleep) being frogmarched out of the township by these youngsters as well.

This experience also had a profound impact on my beliefs. I went on to a theological seminary and there was a professor of dogmatics who had written a paper called *Apartheid, the Will of God* which, quite frankly, I found obscene. At that stage I was into the theology of Karl Barth, who was saying that in terms of the general grace of God those people who have not had the opportunity to meet Christ could still go to heaven. I went to the professor and I said, 'What do you think of this?' He said, 'Barth is a heretic.' I said, 'Are you seriously telling me all those Hindu and Buddhist and Islamic children are going to go to hell?' and he said to me, 'I'm afraid so.' Well, needless to say, that's when I left the theological seminary, not quite sure what I was going to do next. But from then on I developed an abiding revulsion of what I called closed dogmatic systems, whether religious or political or philosophical. I still have this revulsion – to this day – wherever I find a closed system of thought in which the person who espouses the system is the only authority through which you can establish the truth.

Those were my first philosophical forays. After I left the theological seminary I got involved in existentialism: Camus, Sartre, Heidegger. In existentialism, your experience of life determined truth. Of course the dominance of the self became the ultimate source of truth and that's why I've also developed an abiding revulsion to what I call solipsistic or tautological thinking – solipsistic in the sense that you are the only source of truth and if you want to know what I think and what reality is, then come and ask me. And if you don't understand it, that is your problem because I am actually the one that understands everything. It is tautological because you explain your conclusions in terms of your fundamental assumptions. In other words, it's a circular kind of argument, and there's a great deal of that going around in politics.

After I got through existentialism I got into the functionalism of Talcott Parsons. I read everything he wrote until I finished my thesis in 1967. His writing was characterised by a high level of abstraction, conceptual analysis and so on but he was what they would call an expert in functional methodology. The dilemma with functional methodology is that you always explained something in terms of the contribution it was going to make to a system – a functional system. Biology uses functional methodology to a very large extent. Now, he wrote something called *The Theory of Action* and I did my thesis on that and came to the conclusion that it was a massive exercise in what I called teleological explanation – explaining the present in terms of the future. You have access to what's going to happen and therefore you can now reveal what the truth is now – and that is also not uncommon in politics. Apartheid was a teleological system. I would say national socialism is a teleological system. Both of them are redemptive ideologies, promising the chicken in the pot if you vote for them. In the one case you had to be white; in the other case you had to be oppressed, but you were going to be redeemed. So I also developed an abiding suspicion (not necessarily rejection) of what I call systems analysis.

I must just give you a little story about Parsons. When Parsons came out to South Africa I was already in parliament. I had sent him my thesis, and he said a few complimentary things about it. A short, stocky little man. He came out to a conference while I was in parliament and he said, 'Where's this Slabbert fellow?' Now, people like Eschel Rhoodie, the father of the information scandal, did not like me, so they said, 'No, he's not available, he's in parliament.' Parsons said, 'But I'd like to meet him.' So we finally met and I drove him to the airport. I wanted to talk systems theory and all he wanted to talk about was how you grow strawberries. We got to the airport, and we sat down, and as we were talking the waiter came up to me with a book and said, 'Wouldn't you give me your autograph?' and that's because I played two games for Western Province. So I said, 'You know, you mustn't ask me for my autograph. Do you know who this man is? He's one of the greatest minds of the twentieth century. Ask *him* for his autograph.' And he looked at Parsons and said, 'Ja, but did he play for Province as well?'

After the completion of my thesis I realised how little I knew of the world around me. It was all in my head and I began to read a bit of South African history and also about the problems of modernisation. Then I discovered the philosophy of Karl Popper and Ernest Gellner and the Vienna school, and the tensions between positivism and post-modernism, and Wittgenstein. But the issue that got me excited was Popper's insistence on the fallibility of human knowledge, and that knowledge increases through conjecture and refutation. We never know the ultimate truth but search for it through conjecture and hypothesis testing. Gellner was an extreme critic of Popper. Popper's famous work is called *The Open Society and its Enemies*, and Gellner always said that *The Open Society and its Enemies* was written by one of the greatest enemies of the open society. That was his view of Popper. But because of their impact on my life, I developed an abiding revulsion for intellectuals who sought disciples rather than debate, and I still have it very strongly today. I'm not up for recruitment in any sense.

I finished my PhD when I was 27, taught for six more years and went to parliament. I had by that time developed a deep revulsion for closed philosophical systems that reduced human beings to commodities, whether in theology, or economics, or politics, and of course apartheid was a prime target of that revulsion. I had no comprehensive theory of change when I went to parliament and I still don't, today, have a comprehensive theory of change. All that I believed I could do from that particular position was to erode the support of young people for the National Party, so I accepted every invitation I could get to go to Afrikaans-speaking universities and sow as much doubt about apartheid in their minds as I possibly could. The first few meetings were broken up but afterwards they wanted to listen and talk and find out what was going on.

I left parliament in 1986 with the introduction of the national security management system and the tricameral parliament. I still believe tricameralism was the most important source of stimulating internal revolt in South Africa amongst the young people, the UDF, and black consciousness organisations. The whole thing was premised on the assumption of the permanent exclusion of blacks as citizens of this country. It was amazing.

I left parliament and we started Idasa. I had met the ANC in exile a few times before then. One time, I picked up the phone and asked Mr Mbeki in Lusaka, 'How do I get in touch with the underground?' He said to me, 'You don't. They will get in touch with you.' That's how I got to know people in the underground like Ernie Malgas and Stone Sizani, and all the people in Port Elizabeth, Mdantsane, New Brighton and so on, and I could see at first hand the extent of repression and torture that those people experienced. So what Idasa tried to do was to try and explore the boundaries of dialogue between repression and revolt. I never saw myself, had never presented myself, as a great activist. As far as I could tell it was really a hydra-headed animal; there was prison leadership, there was exile leadership, there was domestic leadership and it wasn't all-hearts-beating-as-one and a seamless process of revolt. That's one of the problems I have with what I call invented historiography at the moment: that it was just one seamless process.

(One of the fortunate consequences of having viral pneumonia is that I have been taking time to read again. I read Jeremy Seekings' *The History of the UDF*, Daluxolo Luthuli's and Bopela's *Umkhonto we Sizwe*, Eric Louw's *Origins and Legacy of Apartheid*, and then Magnus Malan's biography (which, by the way, is a certain cure for insomnia). I've read a very interesting book by Ngila Michael Muendane, *I am an African*. His argument is close to a closed logical system. He describes himself as an African, and describes me as a European descendant. For him a European descendant will never be able to understand what an African thinks, but an African can understand European descendants very easily.)

So for me the struggle was not as simple as it seemed. I have enormous respect for Oliver Tambo. The people we met in exile battled, just to keep that show on the road and to see that there was some coherence of action and so on. But if you read Luthuli's and Bopela's work on *Umkhonto we Sizwe*, there was only one serious engagement and that was the Wankie campaign. Chris Hani fought there. Joe Modise was conveniently absent but subsequently became minister of defence. The authors were sent to prison; one went to Robben Island and the other was sentenced to death by Smith's government in Rhodesia (the death sentence was commuted when Mugabe came in). And they have a very sober view of what 'the armed struggle' in exile was all about.

Why do I mention this? Just to say that there's a wealth of new material coming out which we should embrace and explore, to try and understand our own history, rather than fall back again on what I call invented history.

On 9 November 1989 the Berlin Wall came down, and shortly after that De Klerk made his speech on 2 February 1990. Now, a great deal has been written about why he made that speech and how he was in control of the whole thing. I was fortunate to have an appointment with him two weeks after he made that speech. I went to him and I asked him in Afrikaans, 'Now, tell me why did you make that speech?' He said, 'Well, two reasons. I had a spiritual leap'(*'n geestelike sprong*), which is one of those solipsistic experiences that exclude any of us, and secondly, he said, 'I would have been a fool not to exploit what the fall of the Wall has done to the ANC.' It was the collapse of organised communism – he thought he had the ANC at a disadvantage because for him the ANC was essentially an exile movement. He was largely oblivious of the internal dissent and the reason was obvious: he was excluded from the national security management system. Botha and the generals did not like him and he did not like them either. Mandela accused them of having a third force, so De Klerk assumed there must be a third force. He appointed the Goldstone Commission and Goldstone said, 'There is a third force.' So he fired 23 generals and alienated himself even more from the security system.

But President Mandela read it like a poem. He charmed the security establishment. He knew that they were very important, and they actually liked him. I remember asking a couple of generals, including George Meiring who was then the head of the defence force at that time, 'But why didn't you stage a coup, you were powerful enough?' Constand Viljoen kept on talking about his 30 000 men under arms who, at a moment's notice, could jump up and take over. And old Meiring said to me, 'No man, you know we follow the British tradition. We're loyal to the government of the day.' And when I put this to Jan Breytenbach who had started the 32nd Battalion, he said, 'That's quite true.' George Meiring, in his own book, writes that on the day of the inauguration, by chance, he sat at the same table as Mandela and De Klerk. Half-way through the meal, De Klerk leaned across to him and said, 'Don't you think we gave everything away too soon?' Meiring said to him, 'But you never used your strongest bargaining chip', which was the security establishment. And I'll come back to this point again because the evaporation of the security establishment is one of the most phenomenal characteristics of our transition.

RACIAL IDENTITY AND THE INVENTION OF HISTORY

This invention of history is one of the two themes of my book *I too am an African, if not why not?*. The other theme has to do with the use of race as an instrument of policy making and inventing history. When the constitution was adopted on 8 May 1996, the then deputy president, Thabo Mbeki, wrote a very moving piece called 'I am an African'. It was sort of lyrical and very nice. 'I owe my being to the Khoi and the San. I am formed of the migrants who left Europe and found a new home in our native land. In my veins courses the blood of the Malay slaves who came from the East. I am the grandchild who lays fresh flowers on the Boer graves of St Helena and the Bahamas. I come of those who were transported from India and China. Being part of all these people and in the knowledge that none dare contest the assertion, I shall claim that I am an African'. And then the unambiguous inclusive statement: 'The constitution whose adoption we celebrate constitutes an unequivocal statement that we refuse to accept that our Africanness shall be defined by our race, colour, gender or historical origin.' I cannot think of a more inclusive definition of African. So when I say, 'I too am an African, if not why not?' it is because my president told me I'm an African. He told me. There he said it and I read it, and re-read it, and the more I read it, the more I was an African.

But if you go to page three you suddenly come into the Broad Based Black Economic Empowerment Act, and there we find that some say that a black person is a coloured, an Indian and an African. Now white has fallen off, you see, and the African there is a black of a special kind. Nobody wants to tell you what kind of a special black he is, but he's a black of a special kind. And if you then go on and you read the speech that was in *Umrabulo* after the latest ANC congress ... the speech written by Joel Netshitenzhe reads as follows: 'The first objective of the national question is the liberation of blacks in general, and Africans in particular.' So what am I saying? I'm saying: here you have a piece of legislation that attempts to introduce affirmative action or empowerment using the same logic of the apartheid-era Population Registration Act, a masterpiece of tautological and solipsistic thinking. There is no legal definition of a black. There is no legal definition of an African. A coloured is somebody who looks like a coloured. A coloured is somebody whose mother is a coloured and he's obviously accepted by the community as being a coloured. End of definition. Round and round you go, disappearing up the orifices of your own assumptions, all the time. The white ... well, the white is somebody who obviously looks white.

Now, if you then take that kind of logic and you transfer it to our attempts at Broad Based Black Economic Empowerment without any legal definition of the concepts black and African, what do you think the difficulties are going to be? Litigation, litigation, litigation and corruption; you buy your own identity.

The supreme irony of it is that BEE does not even begin to address the problem of economic inequality in this country. The vast majority of people who have no houses, who have no jobs, who have very little services, do not even fall under the privy of this Act. It does not even think about them; it is for all those up there doing business. I am chairman of two companies and I can tell you, we go through the scorecard thing and we find ourselves saying, 'Oops, we'd better do something there,' so that we can qualify better for a tender and so on. It becomes a study in absurdity. That is something I wish we would address and have public debates about. If we continue to define our identities in this fashion then I am afraid we are going to be trapped in the same logic that brought us a lot of grief in the past. I make the point that if you hold yourself hostage to a racist past, you can budget generously for a racist future.

That leads us to the second issue, the invention of history. Historiography. I experienced it first hand at Arabella when I was sitting next to George Meiring, and De Klerk was talking to a group of Palestinian and Jewish young intellectuals. He said, 'Well, how can I explain it to you? First I made sure I had my cabinet behind me. Then I made sure I had my caucus and my party behind me. Then I made sure I had all the whites behind me and then I could afford to release Mandela and to negotiate.' So I look at George Meiring, *en ek sê*, '*George, wat sê jy hiervan?*' (George, what do you say about that?). George says, '*Hell die ou kan maar lekker lieg, eh?*'(Hell, this guy can lie). And that night we had a long discussion about to what extent people were actually aware of what was going on – but it was the clearest case of just inventing history on the spot and explaining how it all happened. The simple fact is that the vast majority of whites were not quite sure what the hell had happened, after that speech. I was at Oxford at the time. In fact, I had lunch with Mbeki the day after the speech and he was not quite sure what the hell had happened either. So to argue that it was all there, planned and ready, is not true. It was an invention.

But then I have spoken to cabinet ministers, Broederbond members, people in the security establishment, and it is common knowledge that they were unaware of the extent to which De Klerk was going to go. They knew that something was going to happen. Albert Notnagel says De Klerk said to him at the caucus meeting before he made the speech, 'I'm going to make a big jump today', '*Ek moet a groot sprong gee vandag.*' Still, they were never quite sure what the '*sprong*' was going to be. But thank God he made the speech. I think it was fantastic. The person who responded brilliantly to that speech is none other than Mandela. Mandela seized the moment. He is still revered as an international icon for the way he handled that whole situation.

So I would say that for me, what I would plead for, is that we must avoid falling into fabricating the past in order to get a good feeling. Let us explore the past because thanks to people like Dr Mangcu and others there's a public discourse being launched in South Africa. People are talking. By the way, if you want to read a wonderful piece about the role of Mandela, it's the book by Dr Mangcu. Wole Soyinka wrote an extraordinary piece there.

Let us not be afraid of talking about serious issues: race, identity, prejudice, racism. Of course let us talk about race. Good gracious me, we have suffered long and hard enough because of race. I, of course, as a European descendant, did not suffer as hard as the majority of people. But still, as an African, I had a deep revulsion against the system of apartheid.

CIVIL SOCIETY AND SOCIAL ORDER

If you take stability as a variable, and place it on a continuum from consensus to repression, you can vary from consensual stability to repressive stability. In societies where you have repressive stability, you very seldom have any vibrant civil society. Since De Klerk fired 23 generals and the national security management system began to evaporate we have had a vibrant civil society. We no longer seriously talk about an army. Who's the head of the defence force? You would have to scratch your head. In my days you would have said 'Malan', just like that. Where is the defence force? What is their role in maintaining stability? You see, it's a different situation. We have a vibrant civil society. Even in those days, when Constand was threatening with 30 000 men to stage a coup, I asked George Meiring about it. I said, '*George, wat van Constand en daai 30 000?*' He said, 'Man, they're not good soldiers.' He said, 'I can tell you now, when Constand came to me and I said, "Yes,

57

Constand, I know about your 30 000." Constand said, "But you know, George, you and I can take over this country tomorrow." I said to him, "*Dis waar*, but what do we do the next day?"' That was his reply: 'What do we do the next day?'.

So that was an acceptance that we'd come to the end of the line of repressive stability. But what it has done is open up an enormous scope for civil society action. And let me not be too blue sky about it because crime is also part of civil society action. As Max Weber would say, crime is simply an unconventional way of pursuing conventional goals. It's riddled with entrepreneurship. But unfortunately it also poses a threat to our stability and our transition. And the question now is whether succession politics in the ANC poses a threat to stability. Is there a general lurking somewhere, an angry colonel or a couple of them? If you look at Zimbabwe, General Mujuru and his lot are maintaining the order there, such as it is. But here we have civil society, we have consensual stability and I am deeply grateful for that – we have some scope for consensual stability.

However, we have an enormous crisis of service delivery. I am not trying to be sanguine about it, but it is an area where I believe civil society can begin to mobilise. Part of the mobilisation to address that problem must at least be public deliberation and discourse. We must not be scared to take on the leadership. If the president says, 'Trust me on Selebi,' I should be able to say, 'Sure, but why must I trust you? What do you know that I don't know? Tell us why we must trust you. Tell us so that we can trust you with absolute conviction.'

We must not be afraid to ask these questions. Why must we reduce ourselves to silent idiots? It is not necessary.

AFRICA IN EUROPE, EGYPT IN GREECE

4

MARTIN BERNAL

In both imagination and reality, Ancient Greece is central to European identity. Since the early nineteenth century, northern Europeans have projected onto the Ancient Greeks all that they like to think good about themselves. They see Greece as the source of poetry, art, philosophy, science, freedom and democracy. They also see its culture as essentially having created itself, through what is called 'the Greek Miracle'. This is seen to have led directly and inexorably to the triumphs of modern 'Western Civilisation'.

By contrast, Ancient Egypt is portrayed as 'exotic' or 'other,' a rich and fascinating culture but essentially sterile and having contributed little or nothing to the mainstream of world history. In my series with the general title *Black Athena*[1] I have argued that both of these images are flawed. Far from being essentially European, Ancient Greece was not pure but thoroughly hybrid, and its undoubted creativity came precisely from that hybridity. Furthermore, the main outside influences on Greece, and those that introduced urban civilisation to the Aegean, came from Egypt and Syro-Palestine.

Opponents of Afrocentrism argue that Egypt was not really part of Africa and stress the fact that it lies on the continent's north east corner. They do not note that the same argument could be used to detach Greece from the rest of Europe because of its peripheral position on the continent.

The Africanity of Egypt can be set out in a number of ways. The first and most obvious is that Egypt is geographically part of the African continent. Furthermore, Egypt has always been connected to central and eastern Africa by the Nile. In this it is unlike, for example, the Maghreb in north west Africa, which for the last four thousand years has been largely – though not entirely – cut off from the rest of the continent by the Sahara.

The second factor is physiognomy. There is a greater physical diversity among humans in Africa than in the rest of the world, for the simple reason that modern people, *homo sapiens sapiens*, have lived here twice as long as elsewhere and diversity develops with time. We know from their remains that, as with modern Egyptians, Ancient Egyptians were very varied both in their facial physiognomy and pigmentation. There has never been a population resembling the red-brown men and yellow white women represented in tomb paintings; it was clearly a convention established to distinguish Egyptians from black Nubians and pale Levantines. The most recent studies of physical anthropology see the pre-dynastic population of Upper Egypt as fitting with those of central and eastern Africa, and that of Lower Egypt as a mixture of these with northern African and south west Asian peoples.

Similarly, the material culture of pre-dynastic Upper Egypt appears to have derived from the eastern Sahara. As the Sahara, previously savanna in the Holocene, dried, people, with their cattle, moved towards the Nile Valley. Later, when there had been interchange with south west Asia, Egyptian culture retained unmistakably 'African' characteristics. For instance, head rests, necessary to preserve elaborate hairstyles, exist in Egypt and much of the rest of Africa but not in Asia. Mummification practised in the early Sahara was central to Egyptian culture and this centrality was not merely material; dissection and the distinctions between the functions of different organs provided themes for the two central Egyptian myths, the murder of Osiris and the scattering and reassembling of his body parts with the exception of his phallus. The wounding of Horus's eye and the use of its segment's eyebrow and pupil to represent the fractions ½, ¼ and so on provided an important model for analysis. The Syro-Palestinians buried their dead and the Greeks burnt theirs.

The fourth link from Egypt to the rest of Africa is that of language.

AFRICAN LANGUAGE FAMILIES

At this point, I shall have to diverge from two scholars for whom I have the greatest respect, Sheikh Anta Diop and Theophile Obenga. They maintain that all African languages come ultimately from one source which separates them from those of other continents. I disagree, believing that while all human languages probably do have an extremely distant single origin, it is useful to distinguish among different African language families. On the whole, I accept the taxonomy established by the late Joseph Greenberg, who maintained that all the thousands of African languages or dialects can be classified under one of four heads or language families. These he named Nilo-Saharan, Niger-Congo, Khoisan and Afroasiatic.

The Nilo-Saharan family is loose linguistically and widespread geographically. It contains Songhai, in West Africa, Kanuri in the Sahara and Nubian in the Middle Nile. Its best known languages are Shiluk and Nuer in the Upper Nile and Luo and Maasai in Kenya and Tanzania. The diverse nature and distribution of the languages in this family indicate that it is extremely old.

Some scholars argue that Greenberg's Niger-Congo family is a successful branch of Nilo-Saharan or at least that they both should be seen as members of a Congo-Saharan super-family. Niger-Congo languages stretch from Wolof and the 'Atlantic languages' in the west to the Nguni cluster in the extreme south-east of the continent. All the major languages of coastal West Africa suh as Yoroba and Fanti belong to this family, but by far the most important branch is Bantu. This language sub-family covers almost all of southern Africa. The close relations among these languages indicate that they spread and diverged relatively recently, probably in the last 3 000 years.

The oldest African language family consists of those spoken by Khoi and San in South Africa, Botswana and Namibia.There is debate as to whether it should include Sandawi and Hadza spoken in Tanzania, languages which share the most salient feature of the southern languages, the use of clicks. The most striking indication of the family's antiquity is that, with the exception of the Khoi's herding, none of its speakers traditionally practised agriculture.

I maintain that Khoisan had a significant impact on the formation of the fourth of Greenberg's families, Afroasiatic.

AFROASIATIC LANGUAGES

Since I am interested in the influence of two Afroasiatic languages, Ancient Egyptian and West Semitic, on Greek, it is useful to examine this family in rather more detail. Greenberg named the super-family Afroasiatic rather than AsioAfrican because eight of its main branches are spoken exclusively in Africa and one in both Africa and Asia. Because of this, almost all scholars agree that the family originated in Africa, though they disagree as to where in the continent it took place. The hypothetical points of origin cluster around the Upper Nile and the Great Lakes.

The language family that appears to have stayed closest to this 'original home' is Cushitic; its languages are spoken around the Horn of Africa. The only national language of this type is Somali. As a family it is ill-defined and is frequently divided into North, East, South and West branches.

Another group of speakers moved west to form the Chadic branch named after Lake Chad. Today the most widely spoken and best known Chadic language is Hausa in northern Nigeria.

Berber is the original language of most of north west Africa, surviving in pockets from the Siwa oasis in western Egypt to Mauritania – and it was once spoken on the Canary Islands. There is no doubt that it is Afroasiatic but how it came from its original homeland is unclear. It is possible that it spread north-west across what is now the Sahara but which was savanna during the Holocene from 12 000 to 8 000 bp (before the present), but it would seem more likely that it or its speakers moved west along North Africa from Egypt or the Levant. This would explain features shared by the three language families but not with Cushitic and Chadic.

The Semitic language family originated at the southern end of the Red Sea, either on the African or the Arabian side and spread south to form the Ethiopian Semitic languages (Ge'ez, Amharic and others) and north across the Arabian desert (then savanna) to the river valleys of Mesopotamia from where its influence spread to Syria and Palestine.

ANCIENT EGYPTIAN AS MIXED LANGUAGE

The last Afroasiatic language family with which I am concerned is Egyptian. It is exceptional in that although it contained a number of dialects there was only one language. Despite its unity it derived from many sources. As paralleled by the evidence from material culture indicating an origin from the eastern Sahara, the closest language family to Egyptian, in terms of vocabulary, is Chadic. On the other hand, structurally it resembles Semitic and Berber in having many triconsonantal roots. This contrast suggests a mixture of both southern and northern or rather Upper and Lower Egyptian languages, both Afroasiatic.

There are, however, non-Afroasiatic African influences on Egyptian. Many parallels exist between Egyptian and Nilo-Saharan and Niger-Congo words. What is more, Sheikh Anta Diop has clearly indicated syntactic structures in Egyptian that are identical to ones found in his maternal (Niger-Congo) language Wolof. He sees these as indications of a single African language family mentioned above. I would not go this far but see the undoubted parallels as the result of the mixing of peoples and languages that took place in the Sahara during the wet millennia of the Holocene, before the proto-Egyptians entered the Nile valley.

ANCIENT GREEK AS A MIXED LANGUAGE

Its phonology (sounds) and morphology (case endings) demonstrate that, fundamentally, Greek belongs to the Indo-European language family. As its name indicates, this family includes, not only nearly all the European languages but also those of Iran and northern India. For more than a century it has been supposed that the Proto-Indo-European was originally spoken in the steppe (now mainly in the Ukraine) and that, therefore, Greek speech if not Greek speakers arrived in the Aegean basin from the north. These propositions seem reasonable. However, defenders of the present academic orthodoxy have used them to assert that Indo-European speaking 'Hellenes' swept in and conquered the hypothetical native Pre-Hellenic population. This also led them to deny the substantial ancient traditions that Greece had received (including most of its higher civilisation) from Egypt and the Semitic speaking Phoenicians in Syro-Palestine.

In my opinion, it is interesting to compare Greek with English. There is no doubt that English is basically a Germanic language. On the other hand, most of its vocabulary derives from French and Latin, particularly in semantic areas of wealth, power and cultural sophistication. Take for example, the contrast between 'cow' and 'beef', 'sheep' and 'mutton', 'hog' and 'pork'. The words for the animals are Germanic because Saxons looked after them but those for the meat are French because it was the Norman lords who ate them. We know this from history. Even if we did not, however, the origins of English vocabulary would permit us to envisage such a situation.

EXAMPLES OF EGYPTIAN ETYMOLOGIES FOR GREEK WORDS

I believe that the pattern of Greek etymologies allows us to reconstruct a similar pattern in which Egyptian and Semitic speakers held culturally or politically superior positions over an Indo-European speaking population. This corresponds well with Greek traditions of Egyptian and Phoenician settlements in Greece and later study by Greeks in Egypt. Rather less than 40 per cent of the Greek vocabulary has been shown to come from Indo-European roots. I maintain that much of the rest can be derived from Egyptian and Semitic.

To illustrate, I will concentrate on a few plausible Egyptian origins for Greek words lacking Indo-European etymologies, with which we English speakers are familiar.

Egyptian	Greek
Dmi (w): 'village, city quarter'	Demos: 'people'
Tnw: 'census'	Ethnos: 'ethnos, people'
Htr: 'yoke pair, twin'	Hetero 'other of two', Hetairos: 'companion'
Id: 'child'	-ides: 'son of'
Mwdw: 'speech, words'	Muthos: 'myth'
Sb3: 'teaching, learning'	Sophia, 'wisdom'
Sdrt: 'spend the night, bivouac'	Stratos: 'camp' (hence Strategos: 'general' and strategy)

NAMES OF THE GODS

The earliest Greek historian whose works are still extant, Herodotos, wrote in the fifth century BCE. He claimed that the Egyptians taught us the names of nearly all the gods. Orthodox scholars of the nineteenth and twentieth centuries have puzzled about what Herodotos meant. I maintain that one should begin by taking him literally and see if there are correspondences between Egyptian and Greek names for divinities who were identified with each other in antiquity. Here are some examples supporting Herodotos's claim:

Egyptian	Greek
Hprr	Apollo (note the double ll)
Pr W3dyt, House of W3dyt (Egyptian divinities were often called by their dwelling)	Aphrodite

Ht-nt Nt, Temple of Nt (the name of both the goddess Athena and her city)	Athenai, Athens
Nsw (royal title of Amon)	Zeus

CONCLUSION

Elsewhere, I have discussed other aspects of major Egyptian influences on Greek philosophy, mathematics, science and medicine, law and justice. Most of these derive from the periods in which Greek scholars and students studied in Egypt from the sixth to the fourth centuries BCE. With the exception of sb3> *sophia* 'wisdom' however, the sample of words, and the divine names given here, derive from the Bronze Age before 1100 BCE. Thus we can see that the impact of Egypt on Greece, and hence of Africa on Europe, goes back deep into antiquity.

UNCONQUERED AND INSUBORDINATE: BLACK WOMEN'S INTELLECTUAL ACTIVIST LEGACIES

5

PUMLA DINEO GQOLA

> Nationalism is a contradictory, rather than coherent dis-
> course: its internal contradictions are laid bare in its female
> figures, in gendered tropes that are inherently unstable.[1]

[I]t is perceived as the norm that men will not only lead [polit-
ical] processes, but also that their participation is never questioned or subject to scrutiny and debate in the same manner
as women's participation or leadership roles. This reinforces
the notion that conflict, politics and peace building processes
are vividly about male power and domination.[2]

> It is one of the ironies of history that the most pervasive
> and total oppression, the oppression of women, has been
> to a large extent neglected by scholars within the ranks of
> the movement. This can be explained, in part, by the male
> chauvinism which has been the bane of colonial liberation
> movements, and also the imprecise terms in which we
> discuss the future socio-economic order we envisage for a
> free South Africa. And yet, the success or otherwise of our
> struggle may depend on the extent to which we are able
> to involve as wide as possible a front of liberation forces
> against the oppressor regime.[3]

This paper moves from the premise that there are various Black
women's intellectual legacies in South Africa and that they are
not self-evident is due to a variety of racialised and gendered
processes that mask, mythologise and delegitimise women's
agency. Women are (dis)remembered and celebrated similarly
across academic, political and other public spheres. On the
one hand, we find women in stereotypical, stoic, mother roles,

67

hypersexualised, passive and supportive roles; parading as the full spectrum of women's presence, they render all other forms of women's subjectivity unrecognisable. On the other hand lie attitudinal and institutional discourses where women's relevance is simply functional and contained in 'women's issue' topics. Both hands contribute to the 'invisibilisation of black women's work'.[4]

In June 2011, as the country mourned the death of the anti-apartheid struggle leader Albertina Sisulu, the bulk of the public discourse referred to her role as Walter Sisulu's beloved wife, the matriarch of the Sisulu extended family, who mothered some of the Mandela children during Nelson Mandela's incarceration, having introduced Mandela to her cousin Evelyn. Although Albertina and Walter are often characterised as a great love story, and Walter Sisulu as an adoring parent and grandparent, his relationship to her was not as prominent in his 2003 obituaries as hers was to him this year. She was occasionally described as an 'ANC veteran' and 'stalwart', but there was little specific mention of her leadership in the African National Congress (ANC), the United Democratic Front (UDF), and the Federation of South African Women (FEDSAW); or of her subversive work against Bantu Education, her multiple spells in detention, or her insistence that women were at the vanguard of various key political successes against apartheid South Africa. Instead, journalists and political commentators jostled to bestow on her the title of mother of the nation, that 'burden disguised as an honour'.[5] She was cited as a revolutionary mother, rather than a towering revolutionary (one notable exception was the statement to the press by the ANC general secretary, Gwede Mantashe, at Luthuli House a few days after her death).

The three quotations which anchor this paper illustrate the barriers to widespread transformative gender analyses of the public sphere in South Africa. These barriers also inhibit the recognition of women's agency in shaping political processes. Meg Samuelson has argued that nationalist projects are contradictory because they are ideologically masculinist and use specific narratives about women to buttress their male-centredness. Paying attention to the gendering of women exposes further contradictions and instabilities within nationalism. For Wendy Isaack, men's political agency is both readily recognised and naturalised. These twin processes do more than minimise women's political activism – they actively delegitimise it.

At the same time, the legislative framework of post-apartheid South Africa is testimony to the successes of women's activist-intellectual and strategic work. The centrality of the Women's National Coalition (WNC) in the process leading up to the dawn of a democracy already suggests preceding processes and patterns of activist-intellectual work. South Africa's post-apartheid gender contradiction is always haunted by the enormous success of women's collective strategies under the kinds of conditions that Phyllis Jordan and Shireen Hassim write about.[6]

My conception of Black women's activist-intellectual legacies comes from Patricia McFadden's work within and outside the academy.[7] McFadden writes of radical feminist praxis as intellectual activity, and foregrounds the experiences of generating knowledge (theorising) and putting such knowledge to praxis. She asserts that:

[c]ritical to the repositioning of feminist thinking within the politics of post-coloniality is the revolutionary act of imagining oneself through the experience of engaging in intellectual discourse. One has only to realise that the very notions that inform our struggle as activists – no matter where we are situated within our respective societies – are the outcomes of an intellectual process that begins at the level of the imaginary. And imagining ourselves outside and beyond the normative idioms and caricatures that have been so effectively manipulated to silence and mute our ideas and visions is the first critical step towards re-inventing our lives and crafting a different future. Every time we step outside the stereotypes that have been so

cunningly fashioned to patrol our imaginations or dull our intellectual energies – a strategy that is central to domination and control – we engage in politics of the mind, in intellectual resistance, and we change ourselves in qualitatively new and revolutionary ways.[8]

McFadden also highlights that intellectual trajectories are to be located in imaginative, activist sites that introduce newness at the same time as responding innovatively to oppressive regimes. Such intellectual activity is crucial to women's activist energies on the African continent, but is not geographically or institutionally bound. Black women's activist strategies demand a certain development of the politics of the mind.

My analysis of 'invisibilisation' is informed by the substantial work conducted by feminists in the academy to highlight how gender is one of the most illuminating indices for understanding South African history. Feminist scholars such as Shireen Hassim, Desiree Lewis, Elaine Unterhalter and Cherryl Walker argue that gender was not taken seriously within the liberation movement and nor was it, under apartheid, grounded in a strong anti-racist feminist movement. Consequently, these feminists argue, while women were often active politically, their activities were not gender-transformative, and they left deep gendered assumptions and behaviour unchallenged. Women's collective defiance under apartheid saw them mobilised as oppressed Africans (in a form of activism that has subsequently been dubbed 'motherism'), or Black subjects opposed to colonialism and apartheid. Even when women expressed an explicitly gendered identity, such identity rarely manifested itself as gender-progressive (feminist).

The feminist scholars mine the activities, and the surviving documentation, of women's organisations, women's marches and activist women's narratives in the public sphere, to distinguish between *feminine* and *feminist* women's political action thus:

[b]oth feminine and feminist movements mobilise wom-
en on the basis of the roles conventionally ascribed to
women, such as their reproductive or domestic responsibilities. However, feminist movements seek to challenge
those roles and articulate a democratic vision of a society
in which gender is not the basis for a hierarchy of power.[9]

Acknowledging that women's political activism often drew
from a combination of feminine and feminist strategies, a
characteristic of South African activism as much as other ar-
ticulations elsewhere, Hassim nonetheless continues to note:

For the South African women's organisations, the dilemma
of autonomy versus integration was particularly invidious.
On the one hand, political resistance against apartheid
was the crucible in which women's activism was born. On
the other hand, women's organisations had to define both
what political purposes they were organising women for as
well as the *form* that organisations should take.[10]

In the 1980s, those women's organisations associated with the
UDF took on a more 'associational' form of autonomy, maintaining some autonomy tempered with work within the structures of the UDF, but this was whittled down, and eventually
gender and women's issues were relegated to the status of a
'sector' within the liberation movement, an approach that still
circulates in contemporary post-apartheid political discourse
and assumptions.[11]

A second strand of feminist writing contests some of the assumptions and foundational arguments outlined above. These
feminists, among them Elaine Salo, Nomboniso Gasa and
Phyllis Ntantala (sometimes writing as Phyllis Jordan), contest
the ways in which feminist consciousness, or the lack of feminist consciousness, are read into historic activism by women.
They argue that such historical analysis erases the multilay-
ered expressions of women's activism under colonialism and
apartheid, and fails to account for the complex ways in which

racism, sexism and class oppression worked, and were resisted, in women's lives. This second strand argues that it is not always easy to label one form of women's political activism 'feminist' and another 'feminine' without due attention to the context and expression of women's collective agency. In other words, what counts as feminist is largely determined by context, as an examination of some women's actions demonstrates.

Salo, Gasa and Ntantala expressly point to the layered meanings that were found in women's political activism from the early 1900s to the late days of apartheid. They also challenge the assumption that the liberation movement was the catalyst for women's activism by pointing to various specific moments of collective women's action – they remind us of a series of women's marches of 1913, 1919 and 1923 in the provinces that had greater success than the celebrated 1956 march on the Union Buildings, important though this last march was. Indeed, attention to a series of marches that begin in the second decade of the twentieth century allows us to see the iconic 1956 march as the culmination of various women's collective activist strategies, and the harnessing of women's political agency in the shaping of public politics.

Nomboniso Gasa's work, for example, painstakingly mines the archival record to show how women's collective action, on their own behalf and beyond, often predated, shaped, defied and challenged some of the techniques embraced by the male leadership of the liberation movement. Gasa uses the various women's marches of 1913, 1919 and 1923 to challenge the often bandied-about exceptionality of the 1956 women's march on the Union Buildings. This feminist activist-intellectual also points to expressions in the records of what can be read as radical feminist consciousness and behaviour by women under colonialism and apartheid. The following excerpt from the Women's Charter of 1955 is an example:

> We shall teach the men that they cannot liberate themselves from evils of discrimination and prejudice as long

as they fail to extend to women complete and unqualified equality in law and practice.

This excerpt presents an unambiguous challenge to limitations on women's agency in any sphere, and it goes further, to position women as those who will set the terms and lead the way in determining the means to complete liberation across gender.

Arguments in the third feminist strand can be found in the very diverse work of Jacklyn Cock, Nthabiseng Motsemme, Meg Samuelson, Sheila Meintjes and Wendy Isaack. These scholars focus on reading the transition from apartheid to democracy for signs of the specific manifestations of gender inequity found in contemporary South Africa.

Cock has argued that the pervasive culture of militarism across political affiliations takes on gendered expression and lies at the root of the high levels of violence in democratic South Africa. [12] Because the transition did not make room for de-militarisation, gender based violence has now become one of the ways in which gender is communicated.Motsemme, Meintjes, Samuelson and Isaack have focused on the ways in which the public discourse of the transition (as embodied by the Truth and Reconciliation Commission (TRC)), and the creation of a new nation, were premised on the erasure of women's experiences, voices and contributions. Meintjes's intervention was part of what led to the special hearings for women at the TRC. Samuelson, like Isaack, argues that disremembering women was constitutive to how the new democracy was ushered in – since the silenced cannot be wished away, the manner in which they metaphorically speak is disruptive. In other words, the existence of gender embattlement remains a haunting thorn in the side of the new democracy that undermines the narrative of a successfully reconstructed progressive nation. Nthabiseng Motsemme's stellar and groundbreaking work on women's testimonies and voices at the TRC has shown that 'the mute always speak', so that the effects of silence and silencing are not always the wishing-away of what cannot be spoken. Motsemme's provocative reading suggests that since 'the mute always speak', the current crisis of gender in post-apartheid South Africa is the consequence of how women's experiences were brutally silenced in important nation-building institutions like the TRC.

These strands are not self-contained and tidy schools of thought, but useful categories for reading the immense amount of feminist material that exists on this topic. Space constraints prevent a comprehensive literature review of feminist intellectual work of the gender patterns developed in South Africa, and as a result the differences within each strand have been simplified to illustrate the broader field, sacrificing minutiae for the broader canvas. All these strands foreground the ways in which race, class and sexuality intersect with gender in the South African public sphere. It is also true that a large body of feminist writing and activism can be seen to draw from more than one strand.

Using aspects from these varying strands in feminist scholarship from the South African academy, then, I read varying trajectories of Black women's intellectual energies, recognising that some of these legacies gesture to more than one classification as either feminine or feminist. McFadden's argument further invites the recognition that feminine political action may have used some feminist strategies. This complicates even our readings as (Black) feminist scholars – as is shown by Anderton's[13] battle to neatly interpret Phyllis Ntantala's (Jordan's) biography as either feminist or feminine.

EARLY BLACK WOMEN INTELLECTUAL ACTIVISTS

Dominant assumptions about how history takes shape in the world and, consequently, the memorying of South Africa's past, speculate that all leadership is masculine. Indeed, the unstated assumption is often that women's activism takes its cue from men's agency in liberation movements and elsewhere in the public sphere. This view condescendingly makes women seem docile and unimaginative, springing into action only as soon as a man decides, or a collective of men decide, on history's course. It is the kind of 'invisibilisation' of women's agency that Wendy Isaack writes against, in one of the quotations that open this chapter.

It is also against this project erasure that the editors of *Women Writing Africa: The Southern Region* compiled an extensive document of women's writing and transcribed thoughts over three centuries. As Margaret Lenta has noted, such attempts are necessary for those 'who are interested in the lives and thoughts of women of the past and present as well as for historians and literary scholars who ... aim to challenge male bias in accounts of literature and past events'.[14] The editors of that collection also see it as an attempt against forgetting, since even women who were once prominent are neglected and forgotten. The accomplished poet and 1920s public intellectual, Nontsizi Mgqwetho, is an example of a woman who faded into obscurity until recently.[15]

Attentive to the manner in which women's lives and intellectual agency can be obscured, the editors of *Women Writing Africa: The Southern Region* offer an array of voices – an important antidote against typecasting and stereotyping. Lenta continues:

> Because they have been customarily excluded from the public life of all groups in southern Africa, the utterances of women which have survived have often been proceeded from extreme circumstances ... *But women have played roles other than of victim ... Phyllis Ntantala's 'The Widows of the Reserves' and Fatima Meer's 'Murmurs in the Kutum' ... and several others, demonstrate how articulate and highly literate women have been able to move into public life through published text* [emphasis mine].[16]

The project of uncovering – and sometimes recovering – women's voices from previous eras is about bringing to the fore the historic variety of women's intellectual agency at the same time that the contemporary project generates new forms of feminist intellectual agency. Collectively, such epistemic work guards against patriarchal readings of history that posit that Black women and intellectual political leadership are mutually exclusive categories, even though it is a historical fact that many important political strategies were thought up by women intellectual activists.[17] Such political presence is neither exceptional nor unheard of. It was replicated across the country in the lives and agency of Black women whose names may or may not be easily recognisable.

This intellectual activism is obscured despite the fact that two decades ago Phyllis Ntantala warned that:

> Women, specifically the Black women, will and must form a central pillar in such a front [against the oppressor regime]. We submit, Black women have no cause to commit themselves totally to the liberation struggle, unless the freedom to be achieved will in turn grant them equality and human dignity.[18]

In other words, women's contributions to the various arms of the South African liberation struggle were characterised by contradictions. (Elsewhere, I have analysed how this 'contradictory location' worked in relation to women activists in the Black Consciousness Movement.[19]) It is important to bear this in mind in order better to understand the continuities and disruptions of women's political and intellectual agency. The trailblazing initiatives of women like Charlotte Manye Maxeke, Zainussa Gool, Janub Gool, Epainette Moerane Mbeki, Florence Jabavu, Sibusisiwe Violet Makhanya, Ellen Kuzwayo, Winnie Madikizela Mandela, Brigalia Hlophe Bam, Winnie Kgware, Fatima Meer and Mamphela Ramphele fused pioneering academic achievement with radical left politics, thereby offering an interesting range of spaces within which women unleashed their intellectual activism. There are many names we can add to this list. Some are Bunie Matlanyane Sexwale, Caesarina Kona Makhoere, Emma Mashinini, Nomboniso Gasa, Thenjiwe Mtintso and Phyllis Ntantala Jordan – to list only those who write about these connections. It has become commonplace today, after African American feminist Kimberle Crenshaw's 1989 and 1991 coinage of 'intersectionality', to speak about the ways in which systems of oppression work in combinations rather than as singular violent forces. These women – and their counterparts elsewhere on the globe – have been instrumental in the crafting of strategies that contemporary women's and other liberation movements use today.

Indeed, it can be argued that when Mary Hames coined the label 'Black feminist intellectual activists' in South Africa to describe current expressions of radical agency by women 'within and beyond the academy', she had cast an eye to the 'herstories' of this development. In other words, while it is sometimes possible to speak of Black feminist activists versus Black feminist academics, some of the most exciting work straddles this divide since many of us in the academy, who are formally deemed intellectuals, continue to engage in activist living. For some of us, part of that political activism lives through the feminism that we embrace within and beyond the academy.

In her discussion of various excavatory projects concerned with women's historical agency, Lenta notes the manner in which (Black) southern African women have used writing as a key strategy to enter public discourse. One of the most enduring sites of Black women's activist-intellectual energy lies in the genre of Black women's autobiography. This is true: consider the path-clearing and conflicted biographies of Noni Jabavu, *Drawn in Colour* (1960) and *The Ochre People* (1963), in which she claims interpretative authority not only over the politics and socio-cultural landscape of the Eastern Cape, but also of Uganda, marriage, civility, progress and nostalgia – and it is equally true of the writer autobiographies such as Sindiwe Magona's *To my Children's Children* (1990)/ *Kubantwana babantwana bam* (1995) and *Forced to Grow* (1998) and of Bessie Head in *A Question of Power* (1972). And there is the momentous contribution of Black women *political* activists to knowledge in this field. More recently, Black women's political autobiography has been supplemented by biographies such as Elinor Sisulu's *Walter and Albertina Sisulu: In our lifetime* (2003), joining collections which present activist women's interviews, as is the case with Diana Russell's *Lives of Courage*.

Although conventional readings of intellectual agency reify the written over other forms of expression, I am in agreement with Susan Andrade's insistence that we pay attention to both 'writing women – middle class women writing ... and rioting women, plebian women engaging in rebellions and uprisings' since such an approach better illustrates 'various modes of participation in politics'.[20] Andrade's slant also rhymes with the blurring of these boundaries which is evident in the auto-biographies of Black activist-intellectual women such as Ellen Kuzwayo, Caesarina Kona Makhoere, Emma Mashinini, Mamphela Ramphele, Phyllis Ntantala, Pregs Govender, Miriam Tlali and others.

BLACK WOMEN'S AUTOBIOGRAPHIES

While much men's activist agency is often characterised through heroic masculinity, it is striking that Black women's activist-intellectual narratives of self are disruptive even of this. In their recurring emphasis on life stories told through the lives of other women, they choose a register that locates them within Black women's worlds, rather than marking them as exceptional embodiments of agency. Speaking to similar concerns, Judith Lütge Coullie has argued that:

> [t]he collective identities we create through weaving out autobiographical accounts into those of others are tied to issues of association and disassociation, power, and social action. In situating ourselves in relation to others, we associate ourselves with them or distance ourselves from them. Through auto/biographical accounts we establish and cement relations to significant others, friends, colleagues, citizens, and comrades and disassociate ourselves from strangers, adversaries, opponents and enemies. In

this manner we construct social realities that open up or close off certain forms of collective existence. Placing ourselves in relation to others also means ranking ourselves in existing status hierarchies. By implication our auto/biographical accounts either entrench or challenge these hierarchies, sometimes also offering alternative ones.[21]

Following Coullie, then, the strategies of self-representation through the worlds of other women, rather than through heroic femininities, is an expression of political will, of association with those claimed communities which make the autobiographical subject as she is. These others that are named, evoked and suggested form a part of what authorises the self-representation. This is the work of destabilising and questioning existing hierarchies. Class difference is often highlighted as divisive, even among those who form part of the same struggle, but the women whose autobiographies I briefly turn to write themselves in ways that destabilise these divisions, suggesting that there are networks forged across class. They also explicitly choose to highlight their lives as those lived in the midst of other similarly and differently marked Black women.

One of the areas in which the distinction between feminist and motherist/feminine activism remains most controversial in academic scholarship is in the representations of motherhood by Black activist-intellectual autobiographers. Emma Mashinini uses an instance where she forgets her daughter's name, as well as the reintroduction to children she has not seen, as indicators of how traumatic torture and detention were. Her reference to Rita, a fellow trade unionist who forgets the location of her home after release from detention, works similarly in Mashinini's text. Because of the idealisation of mothering in patriarchal nationalist narrative, longing for a more stable motherhood has come under sharp criticism.[22]

While mobilisation around their identity as 'mothers' appears to echo patriarchal prescription, part of their apartheid marginalisation – and violent inscription as activists – clustered around separation from their children and the defiance of such separation, even when labelled 'motherist', needs re-examination. As is clear from the representation of self and of motherhood in the autobiographies of two Black women intellectual-activists, Emma Mashinini and the late Ellen Kuzwayo, the claiming of motherhood is complex for Black women under apartheid and cannot simply be read as patriarchal co-option. While both women stress that their longings for motherhood are punctuating moments in their public activism and political leadership roles, it is not to romanticised mothering that they refer.

In *Call me Woman*, Kuzwayo weaves her critique of the contradictory mothering roles placed on Black women under apartheid into a larger telling of her life, as well as an exploration of the lives of variously located Black women. She notes that while white South Africa employs Black women as nannies to white children, the effect is the separation of Black women from their own children. In other words, she juxtaposes the hypocritical mothering required from Black women, as labour in the homes of others, with the elision of willed and chosen mothering of their own children. The insistence on naming the alienation caused as a result of forced removal from chosen family is not a romaticisation of motherhood in patriarchal mode. It is an expression of desire deemed outside the ambit of Black women in apartheid society.

That Kuzwayo's is more than a patriarchal or nationalist yearning for mothering is also illustrated, in her autobiography, in a variety of other representational strategies. She shows how she was circumscribed by various manifestation of patriarchal and white supremacist rule, but it is clear nonetheless that she imagined for herself a different agency.

I am drawn to Barbara Boswell's definition of agency as:

> an individual's ability to act within the constraints of her historical location, while simultaneously critically interrogating these constraints and holding the potential for creatively re-envisioning the social structures which check her actions. It is important to note that the potential for

creative re-envisioning always exists, but is not always realised, or is realised to varying degrees.[23]

Kuzwayo engages in creative re-envisioning when she chooses divorce knowing that societal disapproval will follow – moving to the city, retraining herself from teacher to social worker to political activist in various leadership roles. Not only does she provide a narrative of an individual life transgressively lived, but she achieves it with a critical eye to her larger contexts, which are critically analysed rather than merely narrated. The worlds of Black women, be they liquor sellers or potters, are illustrated with particular detail. It is this value of Kuzwayo's text as archive that Bessie Head articulates in her Foreword to Kuzwayo's biography, when she writes '[b]ooks like this will be the Bible one day for the younger generation'.[24]

This characterisation by Head rhymes with Kuzwayo's inclusion of two lists at the end of her autobiography: of Black women medical doctor graduates, 1947-; and of Black women law graduates, 1967-1982. This is significant in her overall worlding of Black women's lives. Kuzwayo's life story is located within the concentric circles of Black women's drudgery and survival strategies as well as their creativity and excellence. Both ends of the spectrum are part of her story.

This multiplicity is both chosen and inherited. In her 1987 article on Ellen Kuzwayo as the 'first black woman to receive an honorary doctorate from Wits', McKinnell comments on the multiple roles that Kuzwayo takes on: teacher who retrained herself as a social worker, activist and writer. Kuzwayo's response is:

> I suppose much of my input has been that I have lived through history with an acute awareness. It is a history that has largely been covered up or rewritten for our children today, and for many years I felt the need to document the reality.[25]

This claimed agency, which is also attuned to historical marking, is echoed in the contemporary poet Gabeba Baderoon's
poem 'I forget to look', in which the speaker reflects on her
mother's photograph, carried in the daughter's wallet for twenty years. The photo shows a Black woman medical student at
UCT in the 1950s, the first such. The daughter carries it as anchor and because it normalises Black women's achievement
– and it achieves the latter so successfully that the daughter
'forgets' to look at it upon each payment.

At the same time, this photo is a reminder of the hardships
that were overcome by a previous generation of Black women:

> At one point during lectures at medical school, black stu-
> dents had to pack their notes, get up and walk past the as-
> cending rows of desks out of the theatre.

> Behind the closed door, in an autopsy black students were
> not meant to see, the uncovering and cutting of white
> skin.[26]

The name of Baderoon's mother, Dr Nasheba Jardine, UCT class
of 1963, is not one of the names listed in Kuzwayo's book, possibly due to shifting definitions of 'black women', which points
to the perpetual incompleteness of records. A linked text is *A
Life*, the autobiography of an activist-intellectual Mamphela
Ramphele, a Black woman doctor whose name *does* appear
on Kuzwayo's list. Ramphele's multiple lives, as a pioneering
Black woman activist, as a doctor and as an academic amplify
the boundary-crossing narratives flagged in Kuzwayo's text.

The attention to the messy world of the intimate as well as
intellectual-activist agency in the biographies above is also
present in Emma Mashinini's autobiography. Both these autobiographies present the lives of women leaders considered
dangerous by the apartheid state, even if patriarchal nationalist narrative would have them rendered as less effective.

Emma Mashinini's biography tells of the life of a trade
unionist in explicitly feminist register, even though she does

not use that word to describe herself in the pages of her text. As a founder leader of various unions, her autobiography: 'reminds us of a challenge that is often forgotten in the hustle and bustle for national liberation: the challenge to men and women involved in the different facets of the liberation struggle to reflect upon our common humanity and to ensure that in 'building tomorrow today' we pay attention to the triple oppression of women', as Brigalia Bam, then deputy general secretary of the South African Council of Churches, notes in her endorsement of the book on its cover. The similarity between Bam's comments, and Jordan's at the top of this paper, are striking. Nomalizo Leah Tutu's Foreword echoes some of the intricate ways in which Mashinini's text is about the interlocking white supremacist and patriarchal terror,and Mashinini's own agency in the light of this. Describing this autobiography as a 'triumphant record of a woman's resilience in the face of men's oppression ... which followed the writer to her place of work – the boss in the factory, and to her private life – security police who do not respect the sanctity of her bedroom. It follows her to detention without trial – indeed to the bitter end of interrogation intended to break her. Emma does not give in, nor does she give up', Tutu underscores the many ways in which Mashini exercises activist-intellectual agency against the odds. This, like the biographies mentioned above, is not the record of a docile Black women's life. Instead, both within the text and in the endorsements chosen, Mashinini's is marked as an uncowered life.

EMBATTLEMENT CONTINUITIES

The invisibilisation of Black women's intellectual work is not limited to the past. In what follows, I will limit myself to activity within the academy. Feminists in the literary, historical, cultural and media studies disciplines have pointed out, and repeatedly critiqued, the re-enactment of history and political activism as the terrain of masculine heroism, whether in creative narrative or public memorial rehearsal (cf. the TRC) which works to invisibilise Black women, especially, but also other women's contributions to what we know about South Africa.[27] We have also pointed out – an argument Ntantala made in *Sechaba* (December 1984) – how women radicalised the liberation movement at certain points.

There continue to be arguments about the absence of Black women and of Black women intellectuals in contemporary South Africa, but to argue that there are no Black women intellectuals in South Africa's public life is to be complicit with the ways in which our contributions are routinely unrecognised and displaced. This came out quite clearly in Barbara Boswell's response to Khadija Margadie's article in the *Mail and Guardian*.[28] I reproduce part of it in some detail here because of the combination of arguments that need constant re-stating:

> While acknowledging the media's role in marginalising women, Magardie fails to examine her complicity as a journalist and opinion-maker in deciding who is or isn't a public intellectual. Instead, she chooses a hands-off approach, and proceeds as if the media is a value-free conduit that gives equal access to all people.
>
> Where Magardie has the opportunity to lay bare the ideological processes that govern supposedly neutral news values, she declares, instead, that journalists will start quoting 'smart' women 'just as soon as we start knowing who they are'. In other words, women are to blame if they are not heard in the media. And journalists have no responsibility for sourcing and reflecting a diversity of opinion.
>
> Her article comes in the wake of the third Global Media Monitoring Project study being launched in London on February 15. The study, first conducted in 1995, will show yet again that women's voices are systematically excluded from the media. While South Africa has shown some improvement, the playing field is still far from even.
>
> If Magardie is truly interested in hearing a range of women intellectuals in the media, she should stop berating

and do something. She is, after all, privileged in her access to the commentary pages of this paper.

Magardie could start by persuading her bosses to insert one or two women into the exclusively male gallery of *M&G* columnists. Then, she could ask her editors to stop equating 'women' with sex and the body, as they do each week by publishing women's writing under the 'Body Language' rubric. Finally, Magardie could stop reducing women to their 'pussies' and 'tits'.

Let's raise the bar a little higher than mean-spirited misogyny, and start a meaningful debate on this issue.

Like Boswell, I read Margadie's erasure as laziness and unwillingness to look at the many sites within which such activity exists. The journalist and columnist performs on the pages of a post-apartheid newspaper a similar kind of move that later leads to the anthologisation and recovery moves I discussed earlier in this paper. Her invisibilisation is not only personal-political limitation, however; it is linked to the consistent privileging of men's 'expert' and academic opinion in media platforms and to the overlooking of women's intellectual work, even when these women occupy similar academic locations.

Such erasing 'ignorance' rests on the uncritical occupation and use of privileged positions to buttress the status quo. Rather than assuming that women respond or can speak on limited topics and in set capacities,[29] it is important to move beyond the misogynist and lazy erasure of women's intellectual and political agency. Like Boswell, I have listed various Black women intellectuals as part of mapping the genealogies of women's intellectual agency. This should not be necessary, but in the face of relentless erasure, such lists continue to be necessary, even if they are always incomplete.

Contributions made by women activist intellectuals exist along a continuum. Many of our academic disciplines teach us to think of history, to think of human experience, of how individuals shape the world in terms of linearity. Gabeba Baderoon has suggested that we move beyond only reading against the grain, to explore what it means to read the granularity of the archive, interrogating our tools and laying our assumptions bare.[30] Often, she shows, the archive reveals rupture and instability, rather than pattern. Far richer are the patterns that emerge when we probe how women interacted with the state directly, and even with the condescension of Black nationalist male leadership.

We should ask different kinds of questions from history. When more interesting questions are asked about history, then what emerges are connections, disruptions, contradictions and continuities that are not immediately clear. A thorough intellectual project does not immediately latch onto the obvious. Meaningfully mapping Black women's intellectual activism, or being attentive to the granularity of the archive, allows us to extract wider variety and more interesting information through the emerging loops and threads, back into history. This project includes engagement with the shortcomings and limitations of women's intellectual-activism agency.

In the midst of widespread rape and of murderous attacks on young Black lesbians because of their known or suspected sexual orientation, it is saddening to note that sexuality is one of the blind spots of the current women's movement. This is a sobering reminder that, notwithstanding the impact of radical women of various generations, contradictions remain.

CONCLUSIONS

Surfacing the locations of Black women's activist-intellectual energies is a project larger than can be achieved in one paper. It is also an ongoing task that requires further feminist intellectual work. Much of my attention, here, is focused on Black women's intellectual agency within the terrain of the political sphere. Historical reasons account for this: the political autobiography and other creative texts provide multiple sites for women's self-representations. My brief attention to these sites brings to the surface insights about women's intellectual contributions to a variety of spheres, often diminished, silenced or delegitimised in the ways highlighted above in the anchoring excerpts from Isaack, Ntantala and McFadden. Feminist literary scholars have paid some attention to this body of work, elsewhere. My engagement with these texts, here, is with attention to the activist-intellectual strategies and disruptions they offer.

Women intellectual-activists continue to see the connections between intellectual thought and political reality in contemporary South Africa. Many post-apartheid Black feminist intellectual-activists continue to explore the connections between class, race, sexuality and gender. Staying with these intertwined threads of struggle explains the low numbers – but certainly not absence – of Black women intellectuals. It has to do with the fact that the vast majority of black women in South Africa are impoverished. Conditions that enable the existence of Black and black women intellectuals are linked to the conditions under which most South Africans live.

Connections between the sites of power and the disempowerment of women is explored by a number of black women intellectuals. We see the continuums explored, very clearly for example, in the groundbreaking work of Cheryl Potgieter on sexuality, and in Sibongile Ndashe's thinking of how voice and subalternity are negotiated in the South African public sphere. One of the major shifts from the times of Charlotte Maxeke's generation is the assertive presence of Black feminist intellectual-activists who contest the terms of our production and erasure.

The academy, like much of South Africa's public sphere, is generally hostile to the production of even the most moderate feminist-thinking Black women intellectuals, who remain invisibilised because of taken-for-granted assumptions by men about structural entitlement. Many of these accepted experts deliberately occlude how gender works in their analysis of obviously gendered processes such as the presidential race, transnational politics and policies, the economy, and rape trials of prominent politicians.

Reading the granularity of the archive, and attentiveness to the complicity in the invisibilisation of Black women's activist-intellectual energies, is part of the urgent task of intellectual rigour required to transform post-apartheid South Africa into an equitable society.

IDENTITY, POLITICS AND THE ARCHIVE

6

KWAME ANTHONY APPIAH

ACCOUNTS OF IDENTITY

To make sense of what we now call 'identity' in our public and private lives, it helps to understand the central elements that all identities share, so let me begin by offering my own account of identity, which explains how identities work by talking about the labels for them. Take some identity-label (it doesn't matter which it is): South African, male, Catholic, lesbian, Swazi, Swede ... everything I say here is meant to apply to all of them.

My story has four elements: ascription, identification, treatment and norms of identification. Let me now say a little more about each of these four elements, beginning with *ascription*. The criteria of *ascription* are the properties on the basis of which we sort people into those to whom we do, and those to whom we don't, ascribe an identity label. People will rarely agree on exactly which properties people of a certain identity must have. Are people of European ancestry really Zimbabwean? Are Muslims really French? One form of identity politics involves negotiation of the boundaries of various groups. If being a devout Muslim is inconsistent with being French, you might not be able to go to a state school with your hijab on. If being white is inconsistent with being Zimbabwean, then you might not get the vote.

Next: *identification*. When a person thinks of herself as, let us say, Swedish, in the relevant way, she identifies as Swedish. This means she sometimes feels like or acts as a Swede, and will sometimes respond affectively in a way that depends on that identity, may feel proud of a fellow national who has just won a race at the Olympics.

Now: *treatment*. Kindness is a common form of treatment directed towards fellow in-group members: Knut helping out his fellow Swedes. Unkindness is an equally frequent form of treatment directed towards out-group members. Here is room for politics, as people try to use the government to enforce their likes and dislikes. And the politics can be very serious: this is, after all, what apartheid was all about.

The final element of my account is *norms of identification*. To understand this idea is to begin to be able to explain what makes identities so profoundly social. Identities are useful, in part, because once we ascribe an identity to someone we can often make predictions about her behavior on that basis, and this is not just because the criteria of ascription entail that members of the group have, or tend to have, certain properties; it's because social identities are associated with norms of behaviour. There's a joke that you sometimes hear told in Scandinavia about a Swede and a Finn who settle down together one evening before a couple of bottles of vodka, and drink steadily for hours, in utter silence. Finally, around two in the morning, the Swede, overcome by a sense of conviviality and fellow-feeling, raises a glass and says: *skol*. The Finn scowls. 'Come now,' he says, 'do you want to talk, or do you want to drink?' In short, people often behave in certain ways because they think that – as Finns or Brazilians, men or women – there's an appropriate way to be whatever they are, and there are things they ought or ought not to do. Negatively: men ought not to wear dresses; Muslims ought not to eat pork. Positively: men ought to open doors for women; gay people ought to come out; Muslims ought to make the Hajj. To say that these norms exist isn't to endorse them; the existence of a norm that people of some kind ought to do one thing or the other amounts only to its being widely thought that they ought to do that thing.

Let me underscore at once how wide a range of kinds of people fit the general rubric I have laid out. There are professional identities (lawyer, doctor, journalist, philosopher); vocations (artist, composer, novelist); affiliations, formal and informal (Springbok fan, jazz *afficionado*, Dutch Reformed,

Anglican); and so on. There are also relationships that are an obvious extension of the general rubric: you can be someone's father and identify as such, or treat someone as a dad. Fatherhood has norms, such as things dads ought to do.

Now, if this is what identities are, it appears silly to be either for or against them. Either posture calls to mind the animated avowal of the American transcendentalist Margaret Fuller, 'I accept the universe!' – and Thomas Carlyle's robust rejoinder, 'Gad! She'd better!'

'There it is,' Carlyle's point was. 'We'd better deal with it.'

ETHICAL AND MORAL DIMENSIONS OF IDENTITY

But if we are going to deal with identity, it is reasonable to ask how large a part identities should play in our political lives, whether we take politics in the narrow sense of our dealings with the state or, more broadly, as our dealings in social life with one another. To answer those questions it helps to begin not with politics, not even with social life directly, but with the 'ethical life' of individuals. By 'ethics' I mean something like what Aristotle meant by it: a reflection on what it means for human lives to go well, for us to have *eudaimonia* (Aristotle's word, perhaps best translated as 'flourishing'). Ethics, in this sense, has important connections with, but is not the same as, morality, the question of how we must treat other people.[1] Even after we've satisfied the demands of morality – avoided cruelty or dishonesty for instance – we still have a plenitude of choices to make about how to shape our lives. Of course, we all also have constraints of historical circumstances and physical and mental endowments: I was born into the wrong family to be a Yoruba *Oba*, too short to be a successful professional basketball player, and insufficiently musical to be a concert pianist. But even when we have taken these things into account, each human life begins with many possibilities and, in the end, these choices properly belong to the person whose life it is.

What John Stuart Mill called 'individuality' is one term for this. But our individuality is not, in the atomistic sense, individualistic: it is shaped by the available social forms and of course by our interactions with others. Respect for individual-*ity* is not an endorsement of individual*ism*.

Identity matters to ethics, but so does sociability and so too does morality. More particularly, on the side of morality, we have obligations of justice to all our fellow human beings and however important our other identities are to us, we must not use them as an excuse to avoid those obligations. Looking at the Middle East today, we might find it apt to insist that an Israeli or an Arab identity does not excuse you from treating non-Israelis or non-Arabs with decency; apt, too, to underline that it is wrong when, as too often happens, an American treats the fates of Iraqi civilians as trivial when the lives of American soldiers are at stake.

You might object that I count too many things as social identities. But the fact that my account includes things we don't normally think of as social identities is actually an advantage. These other identities are just as important as the usual social identities in our ethical lives and it is important to put the social identities we normally talk about in the context of all these others. The feature they all share, from the point of view of ethics, is that people make use of them in seeking *eudaimonia*, in trying to make their lives go well.

THE STATE AND THE POLITICS OF RECOGNITION

Why do we have such a range of social identities and relations? One answer speaks to our evolution as a social species designed for the game of coalition building in search of food, mates, and protection. This is why we have the sort of in-group solidarities and out-group antagonisms that social psychologists have been exploring for the last half century. But from the point of view of a creature with that psychology there is another equally persuasive answer: we use identities to construct our human lives. For we make our lives *as* men and *as* women, *as* Ghanaians and *as* South Africans, *as* Christians and *as* Jews; we make them *as* philosophers and *as* novelists; we make them *as* fathers and *as* daughters. Identities are a central resource in this process and, in the modern world, the range of options sufficient for each of us isn't enough for us all. Indeed, people are making up new identities all the time: 'gay' is basically four decades old; 'punk' is younger. As John Stuart Mill wrote, charmingly, in *On Liberty:*

> If it were only that people have diversities of taste, that is reason enough for not attempting to shape them all after one model. But different persons also require different conditions for their spiritual development; and can no more exist healthily in the same moral, than all the variety of plants can exist in the same physical atmosphere and climate. The same things which are of help to one person towards the cultivation of his higher nature, are hindrances to another .... unless there is a corresponding diversity in their modes of life, they neither obtain their fair share of happiness, nor grow up to the mental, moral, and aesthetic statures of which their nature is capable.[2]

Philosophers have written a good deal recently about one way in which social identities have figured in politics, namely in what Hegelians call the 'politics of recognition', directing our attention to the way the responses of other people shape one's sense of who one is. As Charles Taylor points out, this process begins in intimate life: 'On the intimate level, we can see how much an original identity needs and is vulnerable to the recognition given or withheld by significant others.' Relationships, he says, are 'crucial because they are crucibles of inwardly generated identity.'[3]

But our identities do not depend on interactions in intimate life alone. Law, school, church, work, and many other institutions also shape us. The most contentious issue has been the role that the state should play in the regulation of acts of recognition. The issue arises because we live in societies that have

93

not treated certain individuals with respect because they were, for example, women, homosexuals, blacks or Jews. Because our identities are 'dialogically' shaped, as Taylor puts it, people who have these characteristics find them central – often negatively central – to their identities. The politics of recognition starts when we grasp that such disrespect is wrong, and one form of healing it recommends is the inversion of insult: taking those collective identities not as sources of limitation but as valuable parts of who one is. And since a modern ethics of authenticity (which goes back, roughly, to Romanticism) requires us to *express* who we centrally are, members of such identity groups will move next to demanding society recognise them *as* women, homosexuals, blacks or Catholics, and do the cultural work necessary to resist the stereotypes, to challenge the insults, to lift the restrictions. Negative norms of identification are to be replaced with positive norms of identification.

For example, an African-American after the Black Power movement takes the old script of self-hatred, the script in which he or she is a nigger, and works, in community with others, to construct a series of positive norms of identification. Being a Negro is recoded as being black, and if one is to be black in a society that is racist then one has constantly to deal with assaults on one's dignity. In this context, insisting on the right to live a dignified life will not be enough. It will not even be enough to require that one be treated with equal dignity despite being black, for that would suggest that being black counts to some degree against one's dignity. And so one will end up asking to be respected *as a black.*This is a demand that others could accede to as individuals, but what can it mean for the state? On one side lies the individual oppressor whose expressions of contempt may be part of who he or she is, and whose rights of free expression are presumably grounded, at least in part, in the connection between individuality and self-expression. (The term 'anti-Semite', we might recall, began life in the nineteenth century as a self-proclaimed badge of honour.) On the other side lies the oppressed individual, whose life can go best only if his or her identity is consistent with self-respect. How, if at all, is the state to intervene?

There are undoubtedly all sorts of things that might be done here in the name of justice: laws against hate speech or verbal harassment in the work place, state education for tolerance, public celebrations of the heroes of the oppressed, additional penalties for crimes motivated by bigotry. But it is important to see that, while members of groups that have experienced historical exclusion, contempt, or obloquy may indeed need new social practices in order to flourish, what they are seeking is not always *recognition*. When blacks in the United States or South Africa campaigned for the vote, they were not asking for recognition of their identity; they were asking, precisely, for the vote. Not all political claims made in the name of a group identity are primarily claims for recognition.

WHEN IDENTITY MEANS GETTING THE SHORT END OF THE STICK

In social life, too, it is important not to pursue a politics of recognition too far, for if recognition entails taking notice of one's identity in social life, then the development of strong norms of identification can become not liberating but oppressive. There is a kind of identity politics that doesn't just permit but *demands* that I treat my skin color or my sexuality as central to my social life. Even though my 'race' or my sexuality may be elements of my individuality, someone who says I *must* organise my life around these things is not an ally of individuality. Because identities are constituted in part by norms of identification and by treatment, there is no clear line between recognition and a new kind of oppression. Here, as with state policy, we should be mindful of what I've called the Medusa Syndrome: the gaze of recognition that ossifies what it sees.

One reasonable criticism of identity politics consists, then, in pointing out that there's more than recognition – often much more – at stake when people ask to be recognised. This resembles the standard Marxist criticism that identities other than class-based ones get in the way of seeing where our real interests lie. There's some truth to this: we shouldn't judge it inherently better to be a Swede than a Ghanaian, a man than a woman; but nobody should dispute that it's better for someone to be rich than to be poor. Where many old-school Marxists went wrong was to suppose that our only real interests were our economic ones. In fact, because our identities shape our aims and our aims help fix our interests, we can have real so-to-speak identity interests as well.

Many people in the United States voted for George Bush in part because they wanted someone in the White House who was, like them, an evangelical Christian. They voted *as* evangelicals, but this, at best, is very obliquely a point about recognition. Getting a wave from the White House may count as state recognition, I suppose, but most evangelicals sensibly don't hang their self-respect on that rather wobbly peg. They were drawn in, rather, by a sense of identification.

This kind of politics is a deep feature of modern democratic life. We identify with people and parties for a variety of psychological reasons, including identifications of this pre-political sort, and then we are rather inclined to support all the policies of that person or party, in part because sensible people have better things to do than work out, all by themselves, what the proper balance should be between, say, VAT and income taxes. It is also because people sufficiently like you may actually pick policies, when they do think about them, that you would pick, if you had the time. So here, as in many places in life, it is sensible to practice a cognitive division of labour. That used to work by creating political identities – left, right, liberal, Socialist, Conservative, Democrat, Republican, Christian Democrat, Marxist. In many of the advanced democracies, party affiliations are less strong than they used to be, and other identities are bearing more political weight. But that's in part because many of the older party affiliations were class-based, and social class as defined by one's work has declined in significance in people's identifications. In that very profound way a new kind of identity politics, based on the declining social salience of class, has been on the rise since the 1960s. And it does not always work out well for the members of the electorate in question. Many of President Bush's evangelical supporters, for instance, may have done themselves a disservice, since George Bush's actual policies are bad for many of the things that matter most to them – health care, pension provision, tax policy, not losing their sons and daughters in foreign adventures. And though he is, I believe, a sincere evangelical Christian, George Bush hasn't done much in changing the law on many of the so-called 'social issues' that his evangelical Christian supporters care about: stopping abortions, refusing to recognise lesbian and gay relationships in any way, and getting lots of mentions for God in public life. In this case, voting on the basis of identity rather than policy meant getting the short end of both sticks.

In America, where I now reside, politicians who falter with their base can often be heard, on the campaign trail, gravely intoning about their resolute American-ness – wasn't it a bit suspicious that John Kerry spoke French? Needless to say, such deployment of national identity is scarcely peculiar to that side of the Atlantic. You may know the jesting Gilbert and Sullivan song 'For He Is An Englishman'. The idea that one should identify as a Swede or South African – that one should have an intimate engagement with nationality as one aspect of one's individuality – is one we mostly take for granted. We find it natural to think that there are important norms of identification for South Africans, for example: things that South Africans, as South Africans, ought to do.

THE POLITICAL CREATION OF THE PRE-MODERN ARCHIVE

We have a picture of the world in which it is as natural to have it divided into a couple of hundred nation-states. But the fact, of course, is that the idea took form only slowly and only relatively recently. The treaty of Westphalia in 1648 essentially turned the Holy Roman Empire into a collection of (largely German-speaking) states, each with its own sovereignty and, in so doing, set in motion a significant shift in the heart of

Europe. These newly independent states inherited the principles of religious freedom established in the Reformation by the Augsburg Confession, which granted each ruler the right to determine his own sovereign religious affiliation. And so we speak of a Westphalian model, where each nation state has its own sovereign, subject to no higher secular authority, independent both of the Empire and of Rome.

But to the east was still the Ottoman Empire, whose building blocks were not nations but a variety of peoples speaking many languages, often living in polyglot cities where each religious or ethnic group governed itself largely by its own rules. Further east yet, Shah Jahan was ruling a Mughal empire that was also composed of many religions and peoples. And in China, the Manchu rulers of the Qing dynasty had ended Ming rule only four years earlier in 1644, taking over a vast territory that, like the Ottoman and Mughal empires was, once more, remarkably internally diverse in language, religion, cuisine and the practices of everyday life.

In our own continent, on much of the northern coastline, the Ottomans ruled; to their south and east, the Emperor Fasiladas had recently expelled the Jesuits from Ethiopia, consolidating his hold on an empire that had persisted in various forms since the first century BCE. In the west, the Empire of Songhay lay in ruins, destroyed by revolts, first by the Hausas to their south and then by the Sa'dian Sultan, Ahmad al-Mansur, from Morocco. In southern Africa, Mwene Mutapa had fallen to the Portuguese a generation earlier; in the Kongo Kingdom, the Catholic monarch Garcia Nkanga a Lukeni – Garcia II – was struggling with secession in Soyo and dealing, as Kongo kings had had to do for far more than a century, with the Portuguese and the Dutch. (1648, as it happens, was the year that the Portuguese expelled the Dutch from Luanda.) But large numbers of people lived all over this continent, as elsewhere all around the world, outside even the nominal control of any state, farming, hunting, gathering vegetable products and honey, and regulating their lives through local forms of politics. Jan van Riebeeck's settlement on the Cape was still four years in the future.

In the story I have been telling, the names of emperors and kings and the stories of kingdoms and empires play a large role. For kings and emperors resonate largely in the archive from which we reconstruct the past. Whether we are speaking of the written archives of literate bureaucracies – Pharonic Egypt, Ethiopia, Songhay, the Holy Roman Empire, the Mughal Empire, the Qing – or the oral traditions of empires ruled without writing like Mwene Mutapa, our archive is shaped by the politics of its creation and transmission. It is simply harder to tell the lives of seventeenth century Africans or Asians who lived beyond the pale of empire. Their descendants may know their lineages and some of their travels and traditions, but without other sources, we are unlikely to be able to tell exactly what the ancestors of the San were doing in the Kalahari in 1648. The very idea of a universal dating system – the idea that we might wonder what people in five continents, thousands of miles apart, were doing on the day that the treaty of Westphalia was signed – is one that would surely have struck those San ancestors as, at best, extremely strange. What would be the point of it? They would plausibly have said – and they would have been joined in chorus by most people in the seventeenth century in most places outside China – 'Those Manchu have nothing to do with us'.

The point is simple: the archive, oral or written is, naturally, a creature of history. It reflects what people once thought worth recording and what other people once thought worth holding onto or suppressing, forgetting or passing on. It is equally obvious that in making those decisions, state officials, in particular, will shape the archive to make its contents reflect and support particular interests. Do we tell the story of Shah Jahan, the Mughal emperor in 1648, as that of a tolerant Muslim ruler of a multi-religious society? Or should we say, as his son Aurangzeb would have insisted, that Shah Jahan failed to act with proper regard for the will of Allah, allowing, as his famous grandfather Akbar had, a flourishing culture of intellectual debate with infidel traditions? It will depend whose archive we look at; it will depend also on our own predispositions. There is an inevitable politics of memory associated with every state, every identity. And modern nation states, ruled by literate bureaucracies and reflected in modern mass media narratives, have memories as profoundly political as any. This is not a fact that South Africans will need to have drawn to their attention.

THE ARCHIVE AND THE MAKING OF THE NATION STATE

I began with the Westphalian settlement, but this did not, by itself, produce the modern nation state. For that a new and crucial development had to occur: the idea of a national culture and identity. The stories with which I began confirm that there have been names of peoples – Axumite, Roman, Mughal, Manchu – since long before the modern idea of the nation state, but behind the idea of the nation state, as Arjun Appadurai has recently insisted, is the idea of a 'national ethnos'. And that is new. 'No modern nation,' he continues, 'however benign its political system and however eloquent its public voices may be about the virtues of tolerance, multiculturalism, and inclusion, is free of the idea that its national sovereignty is built on some sort of ethnic genius.'[4]

The thought is one that was first philosophically developed in the European enlightenment, especially in the writings of Johann Gottfried Herder. Herder forged both the idea of the nation and the idea that the natural political expression of nationality was in the nation state. What Appadurai calls the 'ethnic genius' of the nation, Herder called its '*Volksgeist*': the spirit of its people, and he taught that every member of a people shared that spirit with every other. That spirit found its expression above all in the language and the literature of the *Volk*: its poetry and song, its tales and myths, and in the music, art and literature produced by the common people and by its leading creative spirits. It was in the name of recording the spirit of the German people that the brothers Grimm set out to collect those German fairy tales the world now knows; it was with the aim of recording, preserving and purifying the spirit of the German language – its *Sprachgeist* – that they began the great German dictionary, the *Deutsche Wörterbuch*. It was in the same spirit that scholars began the collection of folk music from Bavaria to Saxony and that they celebrated the poetry of Goethe and Hölderlin. A people's folklore – the wisdom of the Folk – defined the common spiritual or intellectual life of a nation. And a nation, with its shared mental life, was the natural unit of government.

In contemporary language, we should say that a people has a shared culture and that people with a shared culture – the Palestinians, for example, or the Montenegrins – are entitled to live together in a single sovereign state. The collection and recording of that culture thus became one of the central forms of politics, part of what allows us to think of the people as a single homogeneous entity.

So far, though, this is all philosophy; the doings and saying of intellectuals. The material preconditions for the development of this idea of the national ethnos – and its uptake by ordinary people – were complex. But it is worth mentioning two important changes that occurred in the century after Herder.

First, there were great advances in bureaucracy in the late eighteenth and early nineteenth centuries. Recall that one of the most useful of modern words, 'statistics,' originally meant the 'science dealing with data about the condition of a state or community', and came from the German word *Statistik*, which gained currency from a work, *Vorbereitung zur Staatswissenschaft,* by the eighteenth-century scholar Gottfried Aschenwall.[5] With the rise of censuses and statistics, the question of classification and its political significance comes very much to the fore and we begin to hear a litany of modern nationalist questions. How many people in Hungary are speakers of Hungarian and not German or Roma? Surely many speak one or two or three of these languages. Which of those people are *really* Hungarian – not just subjects of the Hungarian state but authentic members of the Hungarian nation?

The second crucial development, one that Benedict Anderson first identified clearly, was the rise of 'print-capitalism': the rise, that is, of a vast industry in the sale of printed texts. Two things became possible with the invention of print: the cost of reproducing texts fell dramatically, while the accuracy of reproduction rose. The text, which formerly had required a great deal of time and money to produce – and had therefore been limited to the possessions of governmental and ecclesiastical institutions and the very rich – was now accessible to a much wider public. That change in audience and in market led to the second new possibility: the vast expansion of publication in the vernacular languages of Europe.

Once a text such as Luther's Bible in German, or the King James Bible in English, became more widely available, there developed in popular consciousness the idea of the community of its readers. Print also created pressure to develop standardised versions of languages like French and German and English, which had hitherto been collections of often mutually unintelligible dialects. And then print made possible the rise of modern mass media in which speakers of a printed language could read of the doings of their nation; in which Britain, or Germany or France or Spain could become protagonists in a narrative of world history. Newspapers and magazines (what we now call the Press) also connected with the new state bureaucracy by making it possible for the state's rulers to address vast national publics, almost directly – or, at any rate, more directly than ever before. And it began the close interdependence – sometimes hostile, often amicable – between a political and a literary and intellectual leadership, an intelligentsia, that is one of the hallmarks of the modern state. This interdependence is inevitable if the nation's identity lies in its national spirit, its *Geist*, for the intelligentsia are the high priests of that spirit. Historians, novelists, poets, philosophers, composers, and teachers all create or transmit the culture that is the nation's essence, its core and its real meaning. Later, with the development of the non-print-based mass media – records, movies, television, the Internet – the intelligentsia are joined by the creators of mass culture and its heroes and heroines, the stars of song, sport and screen, and a struggle for the nation's soul takes place between the old intelligentsia and the new masters of the mass media. But all along, the poems, songs, novels, movies, sports, are all nationally imagined and conceived.

This is the picture that, for many people, takes a great leap of imagination to escape. And the fact that it *is* hard to escape should be puzzling. Literature and music and mass mediated culture and sport are all, in fact, quite trans-national in their influences and their effects. And the history with which I began left us a world in which hardly any nation states fitted the Herderian picture of the homogeneous mono-cultural nation living under a single government. Those few states that do fit something like this have usually been forced into it over a couple of centuries of violent civil strife: the homogeneous nation is the result, not the pre-condition of modern statehood.

Eugen Weber taught a generation of students of French history that as late as 1893, roughly a quarter of the then 30 million citizens of metropolitan France had not mastered the French language: so much for the *Sprachgeist*.[6] As my colleague Linda Colley argued somewhat later in her marvellous book *Britons: Forging the Nation,* 'The sense of a common identity here did not come into being, then, because of an integration and homogenisation of disparate cultures. Instead, Britishness was superimposed over an array of internal differences in response to contact with the Other, and above all in response to conflict with the Other.'[7] So much for the *Volksgeist*.

What makes France French or Britain British? It doesn't matter what you say: language, state institutions, cuisine, the laïcité of the republic, the empire, Protestantism. None of them was ever a very good answer. And since the end of the British and French empires, large numbers of people whose language, cuisine, religion and relation to empire are hardly those of the old imperial centre have entered both countries. Germany struggles with the distinct political legacies of two halves, separated less than a century after Germany first became a nation state – as the *Deutsches Kaiserreich* – at the end of the Franco-Prussian War. It did so without one large chunk of largely German-speaking territory, namely Austria, and without, as the Nazis were soon to point out, many German speakers in the Russian and Austro-Hungarian Empires. Italy was united by the Savoyard monarchs in the mid-nineteenth century but, like Weber's France, contained a great variety of mutually unintelligible dialects. Even now Italy recognises twenty regional dialects, acknowledges the presence of small minorities speaking Albanian, Ladin, Friulian, Greek, Occitan and Südtirolean (as well, once more, as speakers of Somali and Ethiopian and other legacies of empire). It is conventional to describe the Italian taught in schools and printed in most newspapers as '*lingua toscana in bocca romano*' – the language of Tuscany in a Roman accent.

I need hardly point out that if the states of Western Europe where the Herderian ideology was developed do not fit the mould of the mono-ethnic nation state, it is rare to find anything like it anywhere else. India, China, Nigeria: each has scores of languages and ethnic groups. The United States, where most people speak some sort of English, is not a place that could plausibly be described as having a single national culture: everything that is normally said to be American, from McDonalds to Hollywood to consumer capitalism, is found elsewhere as well and is, in any case, not appreciated by all Americans. There are no doubt candidates for Herderian states: I will give you Swaziland (where only 3 per cent of the population is of European ancestry) and Lesotho (though isiZulu and isiXhosa are spoken as well as English and Sesotho) and the 12 000 citizens of Tuvalu (which is 96 per cent Polynesian and only 4 per cent Micronesian.) I will even give you Japan, where 99 per cent of the population identify as Japanese: there are almost as many people of Japanese descent in the Brazilian city of Sao Paolo as there are non-Japanese residents in the whole of Japan. But we'd best ignore the fact that their script is essentially Chinese, their largest religion Indian, and www.ethnologue.com lists fifteen Japanese languages. So even these obvious candidates for the status of Herderian nation state have their complications. By and large, people do not live in monocultural, monoreligious and monolingual nation states and, by and large, they never have.

THE ARCHIVE THAT REMAINS TO BE WRITTEN IN SOUTH AFRICA

That national histories require a certain amount of blindness to reality is not news. The eminent French patriot and historian Ernest Renan wrote famously, much more than a century ago, in his great essay *'Qu'est-ce qu'une nation?'*:

> Forgetting, and I would even say historical error, is an essential element in the creation of a nation, and that is why the advance of historical studies is often a threat to the principle of nationality.[8]

Indeed, Renan went on to say that 'the essence of a nation is that all the individuals have many things in common, and also that they have all forgotten a lot of things.'[9] What's fascinating, then, is that despite this recognition, Renan went on to define a nation in a way that resonates very strongly with Herder's picture:

> A nation is a soul, a spiritual principle. Two things which, to tell the truth, are really only one, make up this soul, this spiritual principle. One is in the past, the other in the present. One is the common possession of a rich heritage of memories; the other is a present agreement, a desire to live together, the willingness to continue to value the heritage that one has received undivided. Gentlemen, man does not improvise. The nation, like the individual, is the culmination of a long past of efforts, sacrifices and acts of devotion. The cult of ancestors is the most legitimate of all: the ancestors made us what we are. An heroic past, great men, glory – I mean real glory – this is the social capital on which the national idea is based.[10]

But where is this 'rich heritage of memories?' Talk of national memory is a metaphor. Nations do not remember; individuals do. The metaphor of a national memory has to be cashed out in the stories that citizens tell one another about the nation, the stories they teach their children, stories produced from oral and written archives whose shape is the product, as always, of choices and decisions, of exercises of power and acts of resistance – in short, once more, of politics.

An example: the idea of the Hindu, as the writer Pankaj Mishra has argued, didn't really exist prior to the eighteenth and nineteenth centuries.[11] Until then, the term had mostly been used by Muslims and Christians of the region to refer to those who were neither. British scholars basically crafted, from a welter of diverse polytheisms, the concept of Hinduism, which could join the company of the three great monotheisms. The ancient texts – such as the Vedas, the Upanishads, and the Bhagavad-Gita –were unknown to the vast majority of Indians. Only after the colonial overlords translated these texts into English and held them up as the scriptures of an Edenic epoch of 'Hinduism' did they acquire the salience they have now come to have. If there was a religion, then it must have its bible, its canonical sacred texts. Once that archive was mobilised, that identity created, it could then be used by an emerging middle class against the colonisers; it could also, in toxic forms, be used to foment anti-Muslim hostility. (Nativism, it is worth observing, is almost always used by one lot of natives to criticise another lot.)

In giving his account of the nation, Renan refers back to the acts of the ancestors – their heroism, their sacrifice, their glory – as well as forward to the projects that the current citizens have committed themselves to pursuing. The forward thrust is a crucial addition, being grounded in what he regards as a current, empirical reality: the common consent of contemporary individuals. But the backwards looking part of the story – the talk of memory and forgetting – risks suggesting that if we only remembered aright and forgot nothing, all would be clear. In truth, national history is a question of what we choose to remember, not just in the sense of which facts we use for our public purposes, but equally in the sense that we choose which facts actually count as ours. This is striking in the case of modern African nationalisms. Ghana was the name of a medieval kingdom of the Western Sudanic region, entirely non-overlapping with the present day country of that name. Nkrumah, our first president, chose to connect the modern state with its illustrious predecessor. It is sometimes argued that this was just a mistake, but though Nkrumah was wrong in believing that the medieval kingdom migrated southward, some of its people surely moved south and that is a connection. Even if Nkrumah had got his facts right, connecting the two states would still have been an act of choice.

In other words, Renan does not sufficiently grasp that it is not the past itself, but the past as currently represented – the stories we tell, not the reality they purport to recover – that does the work of binding the nation. And that means that his theory is not, as he claimed, rooted both in the past and the present: it is, in fact, based solely in the present, in the stories of the past and the projects for the future we share now. What is so Herderian in Renan is the idea that what makes a people into a single nation is always some set of stories and projects that all of them, or almost all of them, have in common. For what, other than a conviction that people share a national spirit, would make you think that everyone in a modern state – typically a large territory with millions of people – is likely to share such stories and projects? If they do, when they do, it is because there are state institutions – most prominently, education and the national media – that feed these stories to the citizens and that invite them to join in the common national projects.

So nationality, for better or worse, has become a salient feature of the identities of modern men and women. However, the content of nationality – its meaning for each citizen – is the result of cultural work, not some pre-given commonality. That means there is place for reflection in it: for working out, together, in the democratic spirit, what it means to be

American or Ghanaian or, given where we are, South African. In doing this you will need stories from the archive: but since, as I have been arguing, it is not the past but the way we narrate it that matters, the fact that the archive you inherit is a colonial archive, shaped profoundly by the separation politics of apartheid does not mean that you cannot use it – and the alternative archives of resistance that the state's archive inevitably generates in response – to construct a democratic nationality. In speaking not of identity *in* South Africa, but of South Africa *as* an identity, we should recall Renan's insight that the nation is constructed not only by its narratives of the past but also by its shared projects. The real place of the nation, in South Africa as elsewhere, is not in the past, not even in the present, but in a future that your citizens will have to try to construct together. You have to work together in democratic dialogue to develop shared norms of identification that will give a core of common meaning to your South African-ness. The South African identity, in short, like that of any living nation, is a work in progress. Its meaning will repose in an archive that remains to be written.

THE GOODNESS OF NATIONS

7

BENEDICT ANDERSON

THE ORIGINS OF NATIONALISM

South Africa is a good place to have a conversation about the goodness of the nation. If one looks at the immediate historical origins of nationalism, in the last quarter of the eighteenth century, one realises that it arose in the context of a wider popular involvement in projects of emancipation. Jefferson's famous Declaration of Independence speaks in the name of 'The People', but this people has as yet no name. The French Revolution had a huge impact in Europe, the Americas, the Caribbean, and later in Asia and Africa, precisely because of its universalist message, not its local 'Frenchness'. In the nineteenth century, nationalism typically was found in popular movements against emperors, monarchs, and aristocracies, and nationalists in different regions regarded themselves as 'brothers' in a common struggle. The same was true for much of the decolonisation movements of the twentieth century. Nkrumah, Nehru, Tito, Touré, Sukarno and U Nu had all grown to manhood under imperial rule of different kinds, and felt their affinities keenly, even when they did not like each other much on a personal level. Only after the First World War, however, did the nation state become 'normal' across the globe with the initiation of the League of Nations.

At the same time, however, nationalism now has a long enough history for anyone to recognise its dark side. Almost all modern nations are divided along the lines of class, religious affinity, ethnicity, gender, ideology and generation. Many of them have behaved very badly at times, to their own members and to neighbours, and have fallen under the control of corrupt, cruel, and/or incompetent leaders. Why then do nations continue to have enormous emotional power, even in the age of globalisation? How can they still be felt as Good?

Some intellectuals have sought to explain this emotional hold by describing nationalism as a kind of secular religion, marked by the same unquestioning belief that the 'religious religions' often command. But this view is unsatisfactory, for nationalist belief is very different from religious belief. Nations want to be members of the United Nations, along with perhaps 200 others; they wish to be recognised and respected by 'other nations' which, like them, have a lot in common, in spite of local idiosyncracies. A United Religions seems quite unfeasible, however, because each religion makes strong claims to 'absolute truth', and most believe they have a universal sphere of action. It is not that the nation lacks a utopian horizon, as I shall explain later, but that this horizon is intrahistorical. No nation looks forward to happiness in Heaven, or torment in Hell. What it fears is quite earthly: the possibility of extinction through genocide.

THREE QUALITIES OF GOODNESS

It is in this historical-utopian framework that I would like to suggest three *loci* for the goodness of the nation, though they may initially seem pretty strange.

The first of these is the Future. The nation-state form is the first in human history to be fundamentally bound to the idea of Progress. Prior to the rise of nationalism, people were accustomed to the idea that dynasties and empires rose and fell. Peoples merged with others, got assimilated, and sometimes were killed off without much notice being paid. It is useful to look at a map of the Roman Empire at its height, stretching from the borders of Scotland to the southern marches of Egypt, from today's Portugal over to Iran. How many peoples mentioned by Roman historians and statesmen have either changed their names or disappeared? In fact, only a very few, which do not include the Romans themselves, have survived. But the Nation's face is turned to a limitless Future, and it expects, under the banners of Development, to keep moving ahead. What is Good about this?

We can get an answer from a strange passage in a famous lecture given 110 years ago by the great German comparative sociologist Max Weber. Most of the talk was devoted to the horrible mess into which his country had fallen. The dominant nobility had lost all ideas and energy, and thought only of clinging to its privileges; the complacent middle class was sunk in mindless consumerism and political opportunism; the workers were politically illiterate and incapable of providing national leadership. After this gloomy analysis, however (analogies to which one find in the press of many countries today) he suddenly said something quite astonishing: 'If ... we could rise from the grave thousands of years from now, we would seek the traces of our own being in the physiognomy of the race of the future. Even our highest, our ultimate terrestrial ideals, are mutable and transitory. We can not hope to impose them on the future. But we can wish that the future recognises in our nature the nature of its own ancestors. We wish, by our labour and our being, to become the forefathers of the race of the future.' By the way, Weber does not use the 'racist' word *Rasse*, but rather *Geschlecht*, which can mean gender, ancestry, lineage and race in the loose way that permits Germans to speak of the human race *(menschliche Geschlecht)*.

The horizon here is uncounted thousands of years into the Future. Weber is thinking about a Future-Germany, which may have no nobility, middle class or workers, and may share no late-nineteenth-century ideals and hopes. But this Future-Germany imposes profound moral obligations on living Germans: they must be worthy of the Future, so that they can be recalled honourably as remote ancestors. At the same time, these uncountable Future-Germans are part of Germany. Though weirdly put, what Weber said is actually replicated all the time in every nation's discourse. We are constantly asked to save the environment and national treasures for ' future generations'; we pay taxes for schools we will not attend and for projects that will only mature after we are dead; we support armies unlikely to fight in our lifetime. If war comes, we may be asked to lay down our lives not just for our fellow-citizens, but for the unborn. Yet between us and the unborn there is a central difference. Most South Africans can think of many fellow South Africans that they hate or despise, according to their social and political situation: die-hard racists, super-violent *tsotsis*, merciless corporate bosses, corrupt politicians... for such people, sacrifices will not willingly be made. But unborn South Africans have none of these characteristics, or any other than futurity, even if one could imagine among them descendants of those one currently dislikes. This is exactly why one can willingly make sacrifices for them.

The other side of Weber's coin is just as interesting. He says that the Future asks us to be worthy ancestors. He himself was deeply ashamed of his German contemporaries, and this shame is basic to the Goodness of the Nation. If we are incapable of being ashamed for our country, we do not love it. It is a shame that can be very valuably mobilised. What comes to my mind are the mothers in Buenos Aires who, year by year, held quiet demonstrations in the Plaza de Mayo on behalf of all the young people who were 'disappeared' in their thousands by the military regime of General Videla. These mothers wanted justice, of course, but what they tried to arouse was a general shame among their fellow Argentinians, a shame in the face of unborn Argentinians. Hence, a good nationalist slogan is always 'Long Live Shame!'.

The second quality of Goodness is to be found among the uncounted numbers of the National Dead. National history books usually foreground heroes of whom everyone is asked to be proud. Of course, there are always national villains too, though they are fewer. Most striking, however, is that the anonymous collective dead are never wicked. Chinese and Korean nationalists were outraged by the regular visits of former Japanese Prime Minister Koizumi to the Yasukuni shrine commemorating all the Japanese who died in modern wars, and one can understand why, given the real horrors inflicted on the two countries in the first half of the twentieth century by Japanese imperial forces. But if one enters the shrine one gets another kind of impression, for it is full of unfinished diaries and pathetic letters written by young peasant conscripts who died fulfilling what they believed was their national duty. Living Japanese see these letters and diaries as moral challenges to live up to the obligations implied by the youngsters' sacrifices.

In other national cemeteries, a different kind of Goodness emerges. The inscriptions on the graves are typically very short, often just a simple name. Viewers are told nothing sociological at all, nothing about parentage, region of origin, religious affinity or marital status. They will not learn how many enemies a dead man killed, or whether he treated his wife cruelly, abandoned his children, or went to prison for a crime. One could say that National Death has cleared his moral books. It makes no difference if the war in which he died was a good or bad war. The most moving monument to the National Dead in the USA is Maya Lin's austere memorial to those Americans who died in what is now generally accepted to be the 'very bad' Vietnam War (what the monument leaves out, of course, are the three million or so natives of Vietnam, Cambodia and Laos in whose deaths those dead Americans played their own small part). When I read about former president Mbeki attending the memorial commemorations for the Boers who fought and died in their war against the British Empire, it seemed to me that a similar process is at work in South Africa. His gesture points forward to a time in the future (two generations?) when even apartheid will be remembered as a 'national tragedy', which must be simultaneously remembered and forgotten by all South Africans. By then, maybe, young Afrikaners will have learned to be attached to the Apartheid Museum and the Hector Pietersen Museum in Soweto. The Goodness of the Nation can only be understood by remembering that the Nation includes the ghosts of the dead and the phantoms of the still unborn, who are, for different reasons, unqualifiedly good.

But what about the third dimension of Goodness? Do living members of the Nation not make some contributions to

the Goodness of the Nation? I believe they do. The most obvious example are 'collective children'. The word 'collective'
must be emphasised. It must first be emphasised because, understood collectively, they can be regarded as the avant-garde
of the unborn still awaiting their turn at human life, but col-
lectivity also allows us to set aside all the faults of real and
individual children whom we know personally or read about
in the newspapers: spoilt, lazy, bullying, ungrateful, disobedi-
ent, drug-addicted, even criminal. The word 'collective' must
also be emphasised because of their peculiar political status
as 'minor' citizens. It is of course impossible to prevent youngsters under 18 from learning about politics from TV and the
chatter of their elders, or from participating in riots and demonstrations. But the key thing is that they cannot vote. From
one angle, this could be regarded as a deprivation, but from
another, it protects them collectively from responsibility for,
and contamination by, the everyday squalors of even democratic political participation. They have no votes to be sold or
bought, they are not part of national armies which may be repressive of the citizens, they have no incomes so no chance to
cheat on their taxes. If they happen to be racists or vulnerable
to mean ethnic prejudices they cannot legally act upon them
in the electoral process. They can not be blamed if this horrible politician is elected, or that horrible political party takes
power.

A kind of benevolent fiction is at work here: 'our kids collectively' are always good, not least because at every minute
they are gaining new infant members, and losing others to
murky adulthood. It is the same type of fiction that is observ-
able in the field of sexuality. In spite of the fact that children
develop sexual feelings very early, and start menstruating or
ejaculating in their early teens, modern nations draw a firm
and arbitrary line between child and adult sexuality such as
the ages at which citizens may marry, or have sexual relations.
Only after 16 or 17 do the children become, so to speak, over-
night 'sexual voters', responsible for the consequences of their
sexual behaviour.

And adults? Even here, there are possibilities of a kind of Goodness. The rise of the inter-nation Olympic Games historically occurred close to the arrival of the League of Nations. They seemed like a harmless substitute for war. But television changed everything, giving a new kind of importance even to intra-nation athletics. The enormous amount of watching time devoted to sports shows us the modern importance of a continuous parade of perfect national bodies – healthy, strong, fast, powerful, elegant, beautiful and often 'winning'. These young men and women are read as synecdoches of the Good Beauty of the Nation, which is why reports of doping and steroids feel so calamitous. But these young beauties pass us like glow-worms at night. We do not see what happens to brain-damaged boxers after they retire from the ring, or the ruined knees of tennis-players and footballers (new beauties arrive to replace them), just as we do not see the Marlboro man when he undergoes chemotherapy. In this way, mortality is kept at bay, and the Nation remains young, strong, and lovely.

THE INCEST TABOO

Another site of Goodness occurred to me some years ago in the United States. If you are old enough, you may remember the calamitous Iraq-Iran conflict of the 1980s. The US, traumatised by the Iranian Revolution's seizure of hostages in the American Embassy in Teheran, became a close ally of Saddam Hussein, and armed him to the teeth (also with the poison gas that he later used against rebel Kurds). By the time of the Gulf War, this lethal friendship had necessarily been forgotten. At that moment I was struck by newspaper photographs showing American warplanes on which the pilots had scrawled in large letters 'Saddam Bend Over!'. In popular language, this meant 'we are coming to sodomise you'. Not long afterwards, Bill Clinton was elected president, with huge popular support in many quarters, but also arousing violent hatred amongst right-wingers, who eventually impeached him. But there were never any bumper stickers reading 'Bill Bend Over'. Why not?

Here it is good to remember the style of personal address which characterises social movements and national discourse. It is the language of Brothers and Sisters. Leaders of modern nation-states cannot address those they lead and rule as 'my children', as monarchs and clerics were wont to do in the past. 'Brothers and Sisters' has nothing to do with a citizen's age, marital status, class position, or ideology but does have a lot to do with ideas of equality and family intimacy. My own belief is that this form of address is underpinned by a metaphoric incest taboo. Brothers and sisters are supposed to give each other unconditional love, but love from which anything erotic must be excluded. This is, one could say, the highest form of Love, and thus a great Good. The meaning of this in the political life of the nation is that citizen solidarity is the good, austere kind from which sexuality is absolutely barred. Individual citizens can have any kind of 'private' sexual life that they want and can legally get away with, but in the public arena this is out of the question. An American citizen can advertize his eagerness to sodomise Saddam Hussein, but he cannot do the same for his own president without violating the incest taboo. He can be a public beast overseas, but not at home.

In this light, it is not surprising that most nations identify their country as the Motherland. This is, metaphorically, the mother to whom we – all of us – owe our existence, our permanent gratitude, and our austere devotion. She is inaccessible to us, but she looks after us all, with a love that is impartial and transcends anything sexual. So she too forms a source of the Goodness of the Nation.

It is quite possible that readers may find the argument of these pages too abstract and philosophical. So let me switch registers.

THE EMANCIPATORY POWER OF NATIONAL RIGHTS

No book on nationalism is more down to earth than Michael Billig's wonderful *Banal Nationalism*. What he wishes to stress is that nationalism is above all a matter of everyday Habit: dull, only semi-conscious, and absolutely ordinary. It is the powerful, almost unseen glue that keeps the members of complex and large societies from behaving much worse to each other than they otherwise would behave. If I could be allowed to extrapolate from Billig to speak of South Africa – but not South Africa alone – I would mention the following:

First are the television weather reports which, day in day out, incessantly nationalise Nature by showing 'South African weather' extending up into the stratosphere, and quite distinct from the almost invisible Namibian, or Mozambiquan weathers.

Second are South African newspapers, which like national newspapers everywhere, have separate sections every day for national news, and foreign or international news.

Third are 'international sports' in newspapers and on television, which nonetheless quietly exclude any sports in which South Africans do not ordinarily participate.

Fourth are logo-maps – maps giving merely the outline boundary of the country without any written information, but instantly recognised by South Africans, who would probably not recognise the logo-map of Burma, Hungary or Uruguay. One sees these logo-maps everywhere, but barely notices them; they are like the oxygen we are barely aware of breathing, but cannot do without.

Though Billig's work is often extremely funny, he is not writing to 'debunk' nationalism, which he regards, in the tradition of the great Norbert Elias, as a profoundly civilising process. He believes, as I do, that it is a mistake to over-value the significance of 'human rights', above the national rights of citizens. The concept 'human rights', with its abstract universalist valence, is too easily used as a mask for opportunist military and economic interventions by world powers, and too simply used to override local custom and tradition. It is also a doctrine which, with all its real value, still has a missionary, top-down smell to it. The rights of citizens make more modest claims, but they come from, as it were, the bottom up, and require real citizen activity for their realisation. And they were central to the original self-emancipatory thrust of early nationalism.

I do not wish to single out the US in any special way. Having worked there on and off for over 40 years I can speak from long personal observation, even though I am not an American citizen. When I arrived as a student in 1958, racial segregation was still largely unchallenged, 'red Indians' were visible only as villains in Hollywood Westerns, women could get divorced only with great difficulty, abortion was illegal and dangerous, gays and lesbians were terrified, and semi-secret minorities were regularly abused by the police and other authorities. Today, the legal structure of segregation is gone and Martin Luther King has his own National Day; 'red Indians' have become, instructively, 'First Americans', and are on the gentle offensive; divorce is quite simple for women and abortion mostly legal; there has been a huge increase in the number and visibility of female politicians at all levels; gays and lesbians are already allowed to marry in some states and the number will surely increase. If one asks for an explanation of these changes, 'human rights' will be quite useless. In every case, the process of emancipation has been based on the claims of American citizenship. 'As an American citizen', Mr X or Ms Y cannot be treated as anything less than any another citizen. And this has nothing to do with American peculiarity, for South Africa's constitution is even better.

WHY ARCHIVE MATTERS: ARCHIVE, PUBLIC DELIBERATION AND CITIZENSHIP[1]

8

CAROLYN HAMILTON

INTRODUCTION

The past – often the site of contestation, frequently harnessed to projects of the present as their justification or explanation, and sometimes pursued for pure interest and pleasure – is the object of continual public, political and academic attention. But does *archive* matter?

Archive obviously matters to anyone who is interested in what proof there is supporting any particular version of the past being promoted, for archive is understood to be the site of the evidence and in the face of such interest it matters whether the evidence is preserved. It follows that archival security matters to those who actively research the past and those in whose care evidence is reposed. Indeed, historical researchers, genealogists and archivists campaign actively for well-managed archives – in South Africa, almost two decades after the transition to democracy, they are ringing alarm bells, raising concerns about inadequate preservatory conditions, poorly-managed institutions, and a worrying lack of skills among archival staff. But does archive matter to everyone else and, if so, in what ways?

In order adequately to pose and answer that question, this essay first unsettles the term 'archive' a little, and then considers the unsettled form in relation to three issues, the identified South African national priorities of ensuring reconciliation, development and social cohesion, in which matters of redress and imagined futures are tied up with each other. Through this focus, the essay offers a perspective on the significance, and the current state, of the relationship between public deliberation and archive in South Africa. It explores the legacy of

119

the archives of the colonial and apartheid eras, as well as the legacy of the concept of archive itself that has been inherited from those eras. It situates contemporary acquiescences and challenges to those legacies in the context of South African democracy that assumes the existence of a public sphere in which citizens participate in deliberation, and it considers the matter of what Appiah, in this volume, terms the archive that remains to be written.

Since the end of apartheid, the South African government has actively convened something that looks very much like a modern-day Habermasian public sphere, filled with institutions and policies designed to promote public deliberation.[2] In reality, however, the operation of power around archive in the convened post-apartheid public sphere facilitates political deal-making, the exiling of unwanted memories, cultural conservatism and nativism, political triumphalism, and an often narrow national project – and it deflects critical debates about the past. Nonetheless, the pursuit of the wider public interest, and of individual needs, in relation to archive and history, does occur periodically. Sometimes this is mounted only fleetingly and with considerable courage in the public sphere, and sometimes in spaces outside what is conventionally regarded as the public sphere. In the face of dangerous political rhetoric that reinvents the past to justify immoral activity, repression and genocide, the archive as custodian of evidence vouchsafes the possibility of alternative pasts and futures.

ARCHIVE, ARCHIVES AND THE ARCHIVE

The essay looks simultaneously at archive and archives, tracing how they are connected. The term 'archive' offers an epistemological and political frame that allows us to bring into view the circumscribed body of knowledge of the past that is historically determined as that which is available to us to draw on when thinking about the past. This is a demanding formulation. It recognises that there are complex historical processes (rather than mere accidents of preservation) that have established that some things are part of the archive while others are not. Some of these historical processes are rooted in the evidentiary paradigm that underpins Enlightenment thinking; others, as Achille Mbembe has noted, have taken a very particular form in relation to Africa, where the archive of academic and public discourse is especially fraught.[3] Historically and currently, this body of knowledge has given, and gives, shape to 'archives', and in turn has been, and is, shaped by 'archives'. The term 'archives' refers to collections or store-houses of preserved historical resources which may be documentary, oral, visual, material, virtual or physical – a definition which breaks from an inherited usage of the term 'archives' as limited to texts, whether documentary or oral. Both meanings are contained within the formulation 'the archive'.

Conventionally, the materials in archives are regarded as valuable sources which, once interred in a hallowed curatorial sepulchre, are fixed in form and content. Even as we express gratitude for the historical accident or deliberate act that preserved the fragments, and value the preservatory effort, we recognise that 'sources' have long histories of making before they are trapped in the archive; and then they are further fashioned, in the archives, as archivists augment and excise, order and contextualise. Sources and archives are also shaped by the ways in which users and readers, through their publications and other practices, reframe the record. In the wake of these kinds of engagements, we can no longer think of the archive as a point of origin, or the contents of archives as embalmed. Every record warrants – as do the archives in which it is deposited – the investigation of its own life history. And in the course of acts of making sources and constituting archives – and in the shifts that ensue – there is as much forgetting as there is remembering.[4]

These acts of remembering and of forgetting within the archive are the effects of developments in changing public and political discourses. Public and political discourses are slippery phenomena without clear delimitation, and the essay seeks to bring into view dominant strands within them, strands which shape official interventions concerning archives and which set up moral positions within public conversations, with effects for the archive. The essay is thus concerned with how the archive is engaged outside the practice of professional history, while recognising that the work of professional historians – whose practice is, *par excellence*, an engagement with archives – circulates beyond the academy in a variety of ways, sometimes shaping public and political discourses, sometimes marginalised by them, and in turn sometimes shaped by them or undertaken in opposition to them.

One strand of public and political discourse which the essay picks up on is the way in which black intellectuals in particular (though not exclusively) are concerned about the biases of the inherited archive. Many South Africans are aware of the weighty intellectual apparatus, including archives, which used science and scholarship to validate the various social evolutionist ideas that underpinned racist policies. Postcolonial anxieties about archive pulsate powerfully but unevenly in contemporary South African intellectual life, and can be discerned in current critiques of established museums, as well as projects and policies for the recuperation of indigenous knowledge, and initiatives designed to foreground self-consciously 'native' intellectualism.

Another strand involves an understanding of the archive that flows from post-apartheid commitments to redress which encompass the role that the archive plays in the way that the projects of reconciliation, development and building social cohesion grapple with apartheid legacies and seek an explicitly post-apartheid mien. Here the archive is a prime resource in arguments for post-apartheid redress. It is also a prime resource in the imagining of the future. Where the postcolonial anxieties about the inherited colonial archive signal a profound appreciation of how the archive of the past is far from neutral, the redress agenda invokes the idea of neutral archives in order to justify its activities. Thus, a critical disavowal of the colonial and apartheid archive coexists with an inert, uncritical conception of the archive mobilised in the service of redress. Both strands are threaded into the national priorities of reconciliation, development, social cohesion and identity. Much, we shall see, depends on how the archive is conceptualised and harnessed in those activities.

RECONCILIATION

The project of post-apartheid reconciliation demands an inter-rogation of the past in order to identify previous abuses and wrongs, the incorporation of their recognition into collective memory, and the acknowledgement and commemoration of those who suffered from them. Across the globe, political and social commentators, acutely aware of the persistent horrors of ethnic cleansing and other forms of retributive conflict, argue that past injustices cannot simply be acknowledged – information about them is required for continuous public discussion. It is vital, they stress, that the events concerned should be open to ongoing scrutiny, investigation and reinterpretation – but the challenge is how to ensure a redemptive future rather than entry into cycles of revenge about cruel pasts. It is only with the assurance that the archives of these memories is both secure and always accessible that the freedom to leave the past behind is achieved.

South Africa inaugurated a project of reconciliation in 1995, driven by the hearings of the widely-acclaimed and internation-ally-emulated Truth and Reconciliation Commission (TRC) but for all its noteworthy achievements the work of the TRC far from completed the project of reconciliation. Indeed, consideration of the work of the TRC draws our attention to areas of the larger project of reconciliation and redress that demand continued at-tention. Consideration of just two of these areas is suggestive of the range of the larger project.

First: there is the assumption that, somehow, 'the TRC dealt with all that'. Because the TRC has come to stand in for recon-ciliation, perhaps too readily, it is in danger of becoming a device that enables a forgetting of the very abuses it sought to uncover, effecting a closing-off of public deliberation and ongoing talk.[5] In

123

certain key respects, the goal of the TRC within its own tightly circumscribed limits of focusing only on gross violations of human rights committed between 1960 and 1993, remains unachieved. Pursuing this line of argument, at least one public commentator has drawn attention to what he identifies as the suppressed desire in the TRC process to erase the past.[6] Others have noted that, for a variety of reasons, the lines of further activity proposed by the TRC – projects of memorialisation, prosecution, extended forensic investigation and so forth – have stalled.

Second: the focus on the high-profile TRC effectively obscures other areas where there is a need for reconciliation and redress. The reach of the reconciliation project in South Africa, and the linked issue of redress, is not limited to the TRC. The Commission's ambit was confined to abuses of the apartheid era, and even within that focus its activities were highly selective. The injustices, suppressions and wrongs of the past, as well as simply some of the peculiarities and accidental turns of history that yet require attention in pursuit of reconciliation, reach back well into the remote past, include the experience of colonialism, and, indeed, injustices, suppressions and wrongs have also occurred in post-apartheid South Africa

Three examples allow us to comprehend something of the fuller demand for reconciliation and redress flowing from an engagement with the past, although the ambit of reconciliation and redress is by no means exhausted by these examples.

Colonial and apartheid deportations and post-apartheid suspicions

The active manipulation – and often suppression – of aspects of the remote past that occurred under colonialism and later apartheid demands critical redress. The remote past needs to become, not a site of idealised romanticisation, but the subject of investigation, public discourse and active debate. The limited serious historical study of the periods before European colonialisation should be radically extended and engaged publicly. It is hampered by the historical deportation of many of the possible sources into sites other than archives as well as by colonial and apartheid framings of those sources which were admitted to the archive.

Colonial administrations recognised that the political ideas and knowledge tools that operated amongst those whom they sought to rule were powerful resources which could be yoked to their own project of domination. They assiduously collected, and archived, information from and about their new colonial subjects, and brought that information, reshaped in all sorts of ways, into play in the practice of rule and into the knowledge systems that underpinned that rule. The abundant and potent materials they found were thus not annihilated but diligently saved, lodged in the colonial archive where they yet lie – sometimes in the very words of those being colonised – many still awaiting recuperation and rehabilitation in service of postcolonial projects of knowledge about the history of the region before the advent of colonialism.

The particular demands of the British policy of 'Indirect Rule' of the colonies developed in the second half of the nineteenth century placed a premium on this kind of research into local practices. While South African colonial archiving practices may have been repeated in other British colonies, the South African material was subsequently subjected to further distinctive processes that flowed from the policies of apartheid, which were founded on archives capable of underwriting the ethnic divisions on which homelands were based, and on ideas of white superiority.

Brimming as they were with detailed materials from and about those being ruled, the archival holdings that were created were strongly biased by the ideological needs of the colonial, and subsequently apartheid, governments and further moulded by the knowledge categories that the authorities brought to bear on the material they encountered and which allowed the authorities to designate certain local ideas as 'myth' or 'belief' rather than forms of knowledge, thereby effectively dismissing some of their central tenets. It was these kinds of moves that underpinned the categorisation of local societies as lower on a human developmental scheme than those of the imperial power – effectively as primitive or savage.

In the first half of the twentieth century, much of the history of the region was systematically deported to the disciplines of Bantu Studies, ethnology, anthropology and, later, archaeology, where it was treated as cultural material derived from what were conceptualised as essentially static societies. Thus, while some African precolonial material was carefully collected by the colonial and apartheid governments, much was excluded from the official archives they established and consigned to museums or oblivion. In this way, many of the experiences of local Africans, and of early slave populations, were never acknowledged as archive-worthy, and were for a long time excluded from being the objects of the authoritative practices of history.[7]

A key technology of rule, the practices and procedures of archiving delivered the documentary basis for control of land, people and resources by centralised governments, and the archives emerged as the site where the politics of knowledge are rooted – a cornerstone of the storehouse model of knowledge. Invariably collections of documents, the archives are also a statement of the dominance of the written text over the potential archival potency of artifacts, landscape, orality and performance. A veritable panoply of devices were developed for containing the expression of, and establishing control over, pre-industrial, often oral, forms of knowledge. In all these ways, and in the face of the immensity of possible knowledge, the archive proved to be a powerful way of separating regulated knowledge from uncontrolled knowledge. The inherited colonial and apartheid institutions brim with materials pertinent to the remote past but they are viewed with suspicion by the contemporary intellectuals who view them as contaminated legacies.

Although pioneering work has been done to rehabilitate oral sources as viable historical archives, to preserve them, and to research and re-write the history of ancient times, the impact of this immense suppression and manipulation still awaits undoing. The writing of the lost histories of ancient

South Africa requires the convening, out of scattered fragments lodged in odd places and unrecognised as sources, of new archival configurations able to support such exercises.[8] It also requires the promotion of methodologies and techniques for the reading of extant colonial and apartheid archives, cultural assemblages and ethnologies, [9] and in South Africa the postcolonial effort of reinstating appreciation and understandings of forms of knowledge that prevailed in ancient times is very different from that in postcolonies like India, where substantial archives that existed in eras before the advent of colonial rule are still extant. Professional historians in South Africa have made gains in these areas but little percolates into the museums and other public domains.

Negations and neglect

A second example that calls for redress concerns the historical negation and neglect of the archive of black intellectual history. Early mission education sought to create a class of educated Africans imbued with the values and knowledge categories of the colonial powers. Literacy and travel opened the door for members of this new intelligentsia to assess and evaluate the world in which they found themselves. Their critiques were expressed verbally in meetings, and in print in both the vernacular and English press that flourished from the mid-nineteenth century and in book publication, engaging with the cosmopolitan ideas drawn from a wide network of intellectual contacts outside the primary imperial frame.

In the late 1920s, the policy of segregation was introduced, driven by the demands of an emerging settler state dependent on a plentiful supply of cheap labour and which needed to establish an ideological basis for its domination of the majority of the population. Segregation placed these intellectual arenas under pressure. Many of the presses closed down. Intellectuals were forced to express themselves in fictional and dramatic forms, mostly in their own languages, rather than in the increasingly censored and monitored spheres of rational-critical debate and in the truth-claiming discourse of history. Bheki Peterson has noted that African writers were often excluded from physical access to the existing archival institutions and they turned instead to oral texts and imaginatively invoked pasts for the resources they required in order to engage in public deliberations.[10] This vital strand of intellectual engagement and intellectual history was doubly excluded from any recognition in the annals of South African historiography and the dominant intellectual currents of the time; first, by what was deemed to be its failure to adhere to the discipline of history as then constituted, notably where these pasts were presented in the form of novels and plays; and second, by the limited circulation of texts available only in particular local languages.[11] Even more insidious was the refusal to accord the status of archive to oral texts. At first dismissed as unreliable, oral texts were then recuperated by professional historians as sources – but their classification as 'oral traditions' or 'folklore', with their own methodologies, meant that oral disquisitions of various kinds were denied recognition as intellectual endeavours in their own right. While a number of scholarly studies on these intellectual endeavours have been published, considerable archival effort and innovation is yet required to underpin enquiry in those areas.[12] Public recognition of, and access to, archives concentrating on these activities is only in its infancy.

Disavowals and lacunae

A third example that gives a sense of the breadth of the work of engaging the past (and the linked archival implications) yet to be done concerns the hidden histories of the struggle against apartheid. These include, but are not confined to, the effects of the conflicts and struggles within the various liberation movements; the stories of the ordinary people involved in small acts of immense courage; the underbelly histories of the turned askaris; the moral challenges that some of the children of apartheid ideologues and supporters offered to their families and peers when they rejected apartheid; the stories of war resisters and of conscripts; and the layered histories of conquest and land dispossession other than those of white settlerism. These stories are sometimes actively filtered out of official archives, and are seldom the object of direct collecting and curatorial energies. In many instances, it is not in the interests of the current masters of the archival institutions to ensure that archives that permit investigation of these topics are preserved and promoted. Evidence for these many stories disrupts the narrative of the ANC as *the* party of struggle and the convenient view of all black South Africans as liberators and all white South Africans as oppressors. Films and works of literature are beginning the work of drawing out these materials into the public domain, themselves becoming archival receptacles for dissonant evidences.

To some extent, the call of reconciliation and redress on archive is particular to South Africa because of the iniquities of apartheid, their continued effects and their presence as an as-yet-immediate, remembered past. However, demands in the USA, and more recently in the UK, for activities of reconciliation around the distant slaving past raise a similar set of issues concerning the role of archive in public discourse. A significant difference in the shape of the ensuing public engagement in these different settings is that the call for engagement is majority-driven in South Africa, but minority-led in the USA and the UK, and one consequence of this difference is that the ensuing public discourse in South Africa allows a direct focus on historical perpetrations, creates a prevailing climate of ongoing ethical interrogation of historically privileged identities, and authorises an active politics of restitution. In contrast, public discourse in the USA and the UK focuses on the recognition of past hardship, the celebration of endurance, the acknowledgement of past wrongs, and affirmative action within an ethic of multiculturalism. Thus, where, in public discourse in the US and UK abolitionists are celebrated (often, it should be noted, in a manner that deflects attention from past culpabilities), in South Africa anti-apartheid activists drawn from the populations classified 'white', 'Indian' or 'coloured' under apartheid, are regularly dropped out of the story of the freedom struggle, a move that feeds ideas of essentialised identities. Setting in place the archive that is needed to meet this fuller demand for reconciliation and redress, beyond the ambit of the TRC, is a necessary precondition for the realisation of the other two national priorities of development and social cohesion.

DEVELOPMENT

While the project of reconciliation exerts an obvious, and perhaps pre-eminent, call on archives to support public deliberation, we do well to remember that the freedom and peace that are the goals of reconciliation entail freedom to move forward into the future. Freedom is a fundamental human right but, as Amartya Sen has argued,[13] and as the South African constitution insists, it is one qualified and constrained by the available political, social and economic opportunities. The maintenance and expansion of freedom is thus both the primary end and the principal means of development.

For much of the second half of the twentieth century, the international discourse about development was essentially that of modernity and was geared towards ensuring the availability of opportunities for modernisation, underpinned by appropriate infrastructure and skills. The rapid economic progress which such development implied was seen to require painful breaks with the past. As a 1951 United Nations document put it, it demanded the scrapping of ancient philosophies and the demise of old social institutions.[14]

By the end of the century, analysts of the problems of development began to re-examine these assumptions. Setting the agenda for what he viewed as the current post-development era, Arturo Escobar argued that the project of development could no longer proceed without a struggle for reclaiming what he termed the dignity of cultures that have been turned into a set of experimental subjects through the implementation of economistic developmentalism.[15] Escobar's critique poses challenges for a country like South Africa because it requires us to unveil the colonial foundations of the order of knowledge (or 'archive') which define aspects of our society as underdeveloped (the successor term to 'primitive'). It also prompts us to explore the potential contributions in this post-development era of modes of self-identification and accreditation in the development of self-capability, as well as the possible contributions of inherited practices and local forms of modernity. These challenges, like the matter of reconciliation, turn us back on the archive as a critical resource and point up the extent to which both reconciliation and development depend on the way in which identity politics engage archive.

IDENTITY POLITICS AND SOCIAL COHESION

Historically, following colonialism, the high stakes around the archive clustered around the question of nation, as they do today. A defining feature of the apartheid archive was the location of the white citizen in the heart of a large, well-organised archive; the allocation to the black subject of a place on the edges of the archive in ethnology; and the justification of the apartheid definition of nation in terms of those positions.

Nationalism was, further, the pre-eminent form of resistance to apartheid, and continues today in the story of an African people historically oppressed and exploited by foreign peoples. Both the apartheid concept of nation, and the narrative of resistance, conceal how some people became identified as African,[16] and how ideas of foreignness, indigeneity, blackness, whiteness, colouredness, and a host of other ideas about identity used to define insiders and outsiders gained meaning and political purchase. For some, the idea of nation is cultural and calls on the archive to endorse one or another idea of authenticity. For others, as Ivor Chipkin has argued, the South African people came to be defined and produced in and through the politics of nationalist struggle. Indeed, for Chipkin, the specificity of the nation lies not in one set of origins rather than another, but in an idea of nation as political artifact whose form is given in relation to the pursuit of

131

democracy and freedom. Even this idea of nation has recourse to archive, as is shown to be the case in Chipkin's recent exposition. As freedom in a democracy lies in the will of 'the people', definition, delimitation and production of 'the people' is at the heart of the meaning of democracy. We see then that it is the possibility of our social cohesion as a people outside the frame of essentialised and exclusionary identities that is foremost at stake in engaging archive.

The meaning of what it is to be modern and African, a core proposition of South Africa's current development agenda, requires intensive engagement with matters of identity and social cohesion. Reconciliation and development in South Africa are currently proceeding through the giving of attention to race, realised in policies of affirmative action, new curricula, black economic empowerment, land restitution and so on. Racial identity remains important in South Africa both because of its capacity yet to account for the shape of South African society and because of its role in the playing out of the politics of redress. However, as Xolela Mangcu has observed, race is also used as a tool for questioning the integrity of critics. It is further used to define insiders and outsiders within the citizenry, for although the discourse of Africanism is also prominent in public discussion, often in ways linked to race, it is a still more ambiguous discourse than that of race. On some occasions, and in certain settings, the category African includes all who live in South Africa and who embrace their position on the continent. At other times it is used as a term that excludes citizens of Chinese, Indian, European, mixed, and even Khoisan descent.

While the liberation movements have a history of ambiguity around essentialised identities, Mangcu has argued that a strong tendency towards de-essentialised identities did not exist only in the explicitly non-racial stance of the ANC – it was also a feature of the Black Consciousness Movement in which blackness was not construed as simply a matter of skin colour (which is how it is used in much contemporary discourse). The exclusivism of that movement was a political strategy that, under the changed conditions of the present, is no longer relevant. Essentialism, Mangcu continues, 'is a particular account of identity. What is different with the nativist discourse of our times is that exclusivism and essentialism are interchangeably all tied up with power.'[17]

In all of these cases, the essentialised identities proposed are open to archival and ethical challenge, but the spaces and occasions of such challenges are limited. The challenge to essentialised identities through the giving of attention to the making of identities is a topic often addressed by historians in scholarly forums. In contemporary South Africa, what has disappeared is the vibrant and critical public scholarship of the late apartheid era that challenged essentialised identities and was routinely popularised and made available through accessible publications. Public engagement of identity claims is today seldom undertaken by scholars, while the cohort of professional popularisers and the so-called alternative publications of the 1980s have largely evaporated.

Two phases are discernible in public deliberation about identities since 1994. The first, broadly coterminous with the Mandela presidency and extending somewhat beyond 1998, was marked by the discourse of the rainbow nation. In that period, vigorous debates about public history flourished. They led at least one commentator, Annie Coombes, to remark on the health and vitality of the prevailing political culture of critique and counter-critique, extending well beyond the academy and revealing something of the extent to which a complex political culture and rich historical tapestry informed contemporary nationalism and defined the South African citizen. Coombes's study drew attention to how a wide range of historical representations using different models of historical knowledge worked in the public domain in construction of national history, in museums, monuments, reclaimed sites, and contemporary artworks.[18]

In the closing years of the century, however, the space of public engagement of identity and the past came increasingly to be dominated by heritage industry practitioners, often working on official heritage projects and policies, and tied into the ideas about identity promoted by government. Many heritage projects were required to ensure their own long-term commercial viability, and found a ready market in the tourism appetite for distinctive 'others', cultural isolates and exotic natives. At much the same time, a new and increasingly exclusivist discourse of Africanism began to replace that of the rainbow nation.

While strongly assertive of an identity as marked by blackness, by oppression under apartheid and by historical indigeneity (though often without including people of Khoisan descent), this form of Africanism was underwritten less by an appeal to a supporting archive and more by reference to the *absence* of an appropriate archive and to the need for its recovery. Some of the recent activity in the area of heritage has been driven by the need to fill this gap. A number of the relevant initiatives were connected directly to the Thabo Mbeki presidency itself, notably the Timbuktu Archive project, prioritised because of its ability to challenge the idea of Africa as an oral continent, and the South African Democracy Education Trust initiative, charged with researching, archiving and publishing the history of the Freedom Struggle. These efforts (along with a range of similar projects supported by the national Department of Arts and Culture such as establishment of the new national heritage initiative Freedom Park) were valuable and urgently-needed archival projects and few would contest their prioritisation. Indeed, recognising and utilising archives outside South Africa marked a break from the previously narrow nationally construed archival frame.

However, the Africanist thrust driving these processes risks effacing the complexity, diversity and contested nature of identity that marked the expressions of public history and culture of the previous decades This threat is nowhere more vividly played out than in the appeals to historically essentialised Zulu culture made by the then ANC deputy president, Jacob Zuma, in his trial for rape, and in the expressions of identity performed by his supporters – claims which stood in marked contrast to strong critiques of Zulu cultural nationalism expressed by academics, as well as by the ANC and its allies before the political transition. In the course of the trial, feminist commentators and activists were rounded on by vociferous Zuma supporters, and critical commentary on the trial was denounced by key figures in the Zuma camp as intellectually incompetent.[19] At the close of the trial, Zuma explicitly juxtaposed loyalty and intellectual commentary, valorising the former.[20]

By mid 2006, public commentators proclaimed a national failure of public debate.[21] Debates around identity, or in which appeals were made to identity politics, had become sites of aggressive silencing and cautious self-silencing.

One of the reasons for this lies in the effects of the long shadow of the injustices of the past, and the linked and ethically-charged demand for redress in respect of the terrain of public deliberation which was for so long dominated by white intellectuals, whether supporters or opponents of apartheid. It is the case that some public commentators (certain white commentators in particular) remain impervious to the need to modulate their public contributions in a manner cognisant of the past. Others however are sensitive to arguments, and vulnerable in the face of arguments, that insist the spaces of public debate formerly enjoyed by whites be filled by a black, African presence – so that recognition of the need for redress has the additional effect of inhibiting the formerly privileged, and the categories of excluded black South Africans, from assuming full responsibility as deliberating citizens. This was particularly the case under Mbeki's rule. It was not just that a climate prevailed in which the ascription of guilt was used to silence some, but also where guilt and, in some cases, vulnerability, led to self-silencing. It further created an opening for attack on non-ANC aligned black intellectuals, positioning them as tools of white interests and espousers of white values. Labelled 'coconuts' (black on the outside, white inside) they were rendered as functionally white, represented as a highly educated elite (regardless of their origins and material situations) as opposed to ordinary citizens, and thereby subjected to the same forms of silencing.[22]

Significantly, just as the crisis in public debate was proclaimed, so too did the tide turn as a small but significant number of independent intellectuals began to challenge publicly the operation of identity politics in relation to public debate. In part, political battles within the ANC which began in earnest in 2006 were responsible for loosening up the space of public debate. In the face of opening and closing spaces of public debate about identity, often dictated by shifts in political power, the need to assert the importance of having the courage and the opportunity to speak at all times becomes urgent. So too, this essay argues, is it important to support a long-term investment in public understanding of the archival claims, and public access to the archives on which such identity debates rest. The ability to debate is dictated not only by the available public forums, it is also enabled or constrained by the available archive.

ARCHIVE, SUBJECTIVITY AND THE OTHER SPACES OF DEBATE

In the 1980s, the leading historian and South African public intellectual Colin Bundy commented on the huge appetite for history in South Africa.[23] It was an appetite fed by backyard productions of alternative histories, and a huge range of popular publications providing accounts of South African history that radically challenged the apartheid version presented in the schools and museums. In contemporary South Africa the lack of interest in history is now much commented on, while the hunger for literature, and the desire to engage the past through novels and memoires, is palpable. Indeed literature and the arts are sites of ongoing complexity of discussion around identity where an archival engagement is often made central. The vitality of discourse in these areas is because they are regarded as 'creative' and as being influenced by affect rather than reason, evidence and history. Precisely because literature and the arts are often sites of experiment and ambiguity, ring-fenced off as a specialist domain, the issues they raise and engage may be matters not as readily admissible or acknowledged as in the public sphere. Indeed, literary and artistic engagement with archive seldom adheres to the evidentiary paradigm which confers on archive the specific role of validation in rational-critical discourse. Artistic and other cultural engagements can involve working in areas that may elude the scope of language or that cannot conform to the logic of representation, and they often use feeling as a catalyst for critical enquiry and deep thought.[24] When contained within the art and culture fields, fields which include critical writing in the form of reviews and essays, these interventions circulate in circumscribed arenas of debate and discussion – but at certain points they may jump fields and enter into other fields, such as the political or the media, and trigger public debates beyond the fields of art and culture.

For the purposes of this essay, the point which is the most telling is the extent to which the current outpouring of literature both reaches into archive for its stories and sometimes even comes to occupy the space of archive, though less with the purpose of establishing truths about the past, and orientated, rather, towards the idea of multiple truths. Complex explorations of identity and personhood abound in novels and forms of creative non-fiction as, for example, slave narratives are imagined off archival fragments, and uncomfortable colonial ancestors, dimly remembered, are called onto centre stage. Works of fiction and autobiography which engage the past feature more prominently on the book review pages of the newspapers than histories laden with footnotes, and some are even best-sellers. This prompts us to explore the proposition that literature today is an important outlet for ideas where public deliberation is under pressure and where the formal archives are found wanting. Just such a situation prevailed in the first half of the twentieth century, when fiction was the elected medium for many black intellectuals who struggled to find spaces from which to contest ideas in the apartheid public sphere. This kind of literature not only reimagines archive, it also engenders public debate in settings beyond the convened public sphere, in what I have elsewhere conceptualised as capillaries of debate and discussion.[25]

POLITICAL FUTURES AND THE ENGAGING OF ARCHIVE

Contemporary corralling of the spaces of debate about the past, and the inadequacies of the available archive, make the challenge of an engagement with the archive that is both ethical and politically astute arduous, but imperative. The defining of some people as insiders, and others as outsiders in terms of the notion of an immutable and authoritative archive, has underlain racial and ethnic mobilisations in the sub-region, with disastrous effects and chilling outcomes. We bear enormous responsibility for how we use the past to shape the future or, as Benedict Anderson puts it in this volume, in order to become worthy ancestors to the as yet unborn collective children. The stakes are high: archive at once produces and destabilises nation, and the challenge to the worthy ancestor is to proceed in knowledge of the power of archive. The worthy ancestor also bears a responsibility to ensure that the archives which are the storehouses of materials from and about the past are cared for and enhanced. But all is not well in the institutions charged with this responsibility.

South Africa's post-apartheid national archival system was inaugurated in law when the National Archives of South Africa Act (NASAA) came into operation in January 1997. It was designed to set in place a new national archival system for South Africa capable of serving the public at large, rather than a racially-exclusive ruling elite. The stated aims of the legislation and linked policy initiatives were to create space for voices previously excluded, to make the processes of constituting the archive both transparent and accountable, to open the archive according to the principles of 'freedom of information', to overcome systemic barriers to accessing the archive, to call into being new publics for archives, to ensure that public archives audit state record-keeping, and to foster synergies between the intersecting archival, museum, library and heritage terrains.

In practice, the processes of opening the archive that were envisaged in the initial policy documents and underpinning the legislation have stalled. The post-apartheid archival effort has largely been limited to transforming the racial composition of archives staff, noting the bias of the inherited archive, and safeguarding state interests in suppressing aspects of the record deemed sensitive. The inclusion of voices previously excluded has been confined to a handful of oral history projects and intensive efforts to preserve the record of the freedom struggle, pre-eminently that of the ANC. It has also included the recognition and valorisation of indigenous knowledge, installing an assumption of continuity between various contemporary forms and those of the remote past.

The records of government itself are, in many instances, neither securely preserved nor readily accessible. Key aspects of the record of the apartheid regime remain out of public reach.[26] Even records generated *after* the transition to democracy are fettered; for example, the record of the Truth and Reconciliation Commission – which the Commission recommended be made available for public consultation – is not readily accessible despite countless interventions by memory activists and lobby groups, legal challenges and high-profile press campaigns. More generally, the post-1994 government has failed adequately to resource the national archival system and to prioritise and valorise practices of record-keeping in government departments.[27] The Promotion of Access to Information Act of 2000 was designed to ensure reasonable access to information but has been used actively to frustrate such access.

In some cases official records are in physical danger. The records of the former homelands are especially vulnerable, often housed in inadequate storage facilities, and in many cases there is no reliable audit of their whereabouts.[28] In the absence of firm electronic records policies and protocols, contemporary electronic records are at even greater risk of evaporating completely.

To what extent are these problems of accessibility and security of the record specific to South Africa, marking the South African archive as different from others internationally? In part they are due to a continuation of the apartheid mentality of secrecy and guardedness. They also flow from the negotiated settlement that led to the transition to democracy in which secret political compromises prevailed, requiring ongoing archival suppressions. They are a hallmark of a young democracy in which the culture of accountability through record-keeping is not entrenched. In addition, much of the available record is tainted because of its earlier role in underpinning oppression.

In the archival institutions of today the appreciation of past records assemblages is limited because of the repressive circumstances of their making, attitudes that prevail despite the many historical studies which make effective critical use of those archives, and which themselves fuel postcolonial critique. Few archival professionals have the skills to reposition the colonial and apartheid archival legacy and to inaugurate policies and projects that challenge or reshape its disgraced elements and foster an appreciation of the wealth of information which they contain over and beyond the intentions of their architects.

In addition, all state archives are primarily concerned with preserving the record of government, but, as an arm of government, are vulnerable to political pressure from those in power to order to safeguard their interests, sometimes at the expense of the public good. The acute resource shortages that dog almost all the archival repositories are a result of limited recognition among politicians and state officials – and indeed the public at large – of the potential of these and other archives in helping South Africans deal with the past, understand the present and imagine the future.

The issues of access and security raised here suggest powerfully the extent to which the archives, seemingly neutral spaces of repository and care are, rather, always configurations of power. They are politically saturated, historically contingent and ethically charged. Challenging the appearance of neutrality, reflecting on the operation of power in the archives, and modulating and inflecting that power with the concerns of the powerless or the marginalised is the corollary of a responsible recognition of power in the archives, and a condition of freedom. While the combination of these conditions is particular to South Africa, the record everywhere is involved in the operation of power. At the same time, as this essay shows, the agendas of power that give shape to the archives require not only abundant information about those whom they seek to control, but control and the exertion of power themselves often depend on systems based on well-organised records.

Informed public deliberation about the past that underpins reconciliation, development and identity politics requires more than security and open access. It also requires intensive contextualising of all archives, the augmentation of one-sided records with additional materials, in some instances the creation of archives where no formally recognised records currently exist, training for archivists in new protocols and procedures for recognising and inaugurating archives, and for documenting life histories of the records themselves; enhanced opportunities for non-specialist users to develop new techniques of re-reading old archives, in accessing archival materials in new forms and places.

But the interventions required go beyond matters of archival practices to engage the very concept of archive that post-apartheid South Africa has inherited, and to redefine it in a way that frees it from its colonial and apartheid heritage, meanings and functions. If archival practices constitute a powerful technology of rule, and if that rule is asserted through control of access to the archive – in the sense of who uses the archive and what goes into it – as well as control over the form that the materials take, then in the context of a change of political power, say from a totalitarian regime to a democratic one, an endorsement of the archive of the new power is not a sufficiently responsible recognition of the power of the archive.

The archive needs to have its certitudes questioned continually, and to be subjected to the question of difference. It needs to be drawn into the public domain and to be engaged in dialogues which – if they are potentially productive – may upend its structure and disrupt its conventions. Such dialogues require that the many publics of archive are vigilant in ensuring that in every invocation of archive the operations of power involved are always interrogated. There is pressing need to promote archive as a space that excludes no one, and to refuse to limit the archive to a place of recovery of original propriety. In short, it is vital that citizens actively engage archive.

Archive as a politically significant site of dialogue underpinned the establishment of the Nelson Mandela Foundation's Centre of Memory and Dialogue. An initial expectation of a project so-labelled is one of the commemoration of a freedom struggle and a 'lest we forget' initiative. The Centre, however, perhaps unexpectedly, makes central to its endeavour the project of dialogue for justice, a project that involves facilitating dialogue around politically-charged memories and filling politically-charged gaps in the archival record in the course of dialogue rather than through authoritative and appropriative collection practices. The Centre seeks to enable the collective negotiation of memory and, more specifically, to involve voices from society's margins in that collective negotiation. It also tries to ensure that collective memories thus negotiated are not consigned to oblivion, but continue to find a place in public deliberation. At the heart of the project lies a concept of the archive as profoundly public, ever opening, never fixed, respecting story, inviting multiple engagements and seeking freedom from the meta-narratives of power.

In the introduction to a book of essays on archives and justice in South Africa, Verne Harris, a former deputy director of the National Archives and currently project manager at the Centre, proposes the centrality of 'Reaching for Hospitality' in archival engagement. He describes this as 'a hospitality to what is outside the boundary, to what is "other"'.[29] For Harris this hospitality is primarily directed at ways of knowing archives that are 'other' to the dominant discourses in Western, English-language archive. Harris indicates that this means recognising that the record (his preferred term) is always in the process of being made and of being determined by relations of power. This recognition creates an ethical demand for the call of justice. The hospitality that he argues for is thus not simply a hospitality to ideas of archive that are outside the boundary, but also to those excluded, marginalised and silenced by prevailing relations of power and its engagement with archive. Far from being a retreat from the hurly burly of South African realities, the Foundation's shift is motivated, it seems, by a need to work actively in defence of democracy.

Indeed, there are a handful of NGOs in South Africa that similarly have grasped what is at stake around archive. Organisations and institutions such as the South African History Archive, Open Democracy Advice Centre, the District Six Museum, History Workshop, the Centre for Popular Memory and the Archival Platform, among others, are themselves not primarily archival repositories (although some have considerable holdings). They are perhaps best understood as activists operating in the archival field, seeking, variously, to ensure that new kinds of archives are established, that underrepresented areas in archival collections receive attention, that open access to archives is protected, that attention is drawn to the operations of power in the archive, and that that power is used to serve the ends of justice

To engage archive, then, is firstly to conceptualise it as open and shifting and simultaneously to value its preservatory commitments, and secondly to explore its manifold powers. In contemporary South Africa, the archive that holds sway in the convened public sphere is inert and either authoritative or discredited. It confounds the postcolonial critique of inherited colonial epistemology, evacuates the project for the critical exploration of indigenous knowledge, underpins cultural conservatism, inhibits active citizenship in democracy and disables the postcolonial contribution to the imagining and fashioning of a new modernity. Fortunately, it is a concept of archive that is contested, sometimes within the political sphere and sometimes in unacknowledged spaces of public deliberation.[30]

Traces of the past are treasures, and fragments of past lives, even suspect lives, are rare materials. Appreciation of them requires a passionate commitment that is mindful of their powers. Even as we recognise and value these traces, the worthy ancestor must remain vigilant in the protection of the freedom to transcend the past, and endlessly to engage the archive.

PREFACE

1   Aimé Césaire *Une tempête d'après de Shakespeare.*
2   Benedict Anderson (1991) *Imagined Communities: Reflections on the Origin and Spread of Nationalism.* London: Verso.
3   Eric Hobsbawm (1994) *The Age of Extremes, The Short Twentieth Century, 1914-1991*, London: Little, Brown.

CHAPTER ONE   *Evidentiary Genocide*

1   Desmond Tutu (2001) Foreword, in Mac Maharaj (Ed.) *Reflections in Prison,* Johannesburg: Struik.
2   Milan Kundera (1996) *The Book of Laughter and Forgetting*, London: HarperCollins.
3   The ANC critique of the 1976 uprisings was contained in the exiled ANC's official publication, *Sechab*a, August, 1976
4   Xolela Mangcu 'Il Duce, Step Aside, A Fascist Fire Rages In Malema', *City Press*, April 2010.
5   Milan Kundera, op.cit. page 4.
6   Robert Fatton (1986) *Black Consciousness in South Africa: The Dialectics of White Resistance to White Supremacy*, Albany: State University of New York.
7   I asked Barney Pityana to write this as part of my research on Steve Biko's biography.
8   Xolela Mangcu (1993) From social movements to planning, Cornell Working Papers.
9   Anthony Sampson (1999) *Mandela, the Authorized Biography*, Johannesburg: Jonathan Ball.
10   I described Mbeki's racial insider-outsider politics in my 2008 book *To the Brink: The State of Democracy in South Africa*, Scottsville: UKZN Press.

11 Ronald Suresh Roberts (2007) *Fit to Govern, the Native Intelligence of Thabo Mbeki*, Johannesburg: STE Publishers.

12 Steve Biko (1978) *I Write What I Like*, London: Bowerdean.

13 CB Macpherson (1962) *The Theory of Possessive Individualissm*, Oxford: Oxford University Press.

14 Benjamin Barber (1998) *A Passion for Democracy*, New Jersey: Princeton University Press.

15 For the influence of Fanon on Biko see also Gail Gerhart (1978) *Black Power in South Africa: The Evolution of an Ideology*, Berkeley: University of California Press; Sam Nolutshungu (1982) *Changing South Africa: Political Considerations*, Albany: Suny Press; and Barney Pityana's chapter in H van der Merwe and D Welsh (Eds.) (1972) *Student Perspectives in South Africa*, Cape Town: David Philip.

16 Nigel Gibson (1977-78) Introduction, Black Consciousness, Centre for Civil Society Research Report No.18: 9.

17 Biko, interview with Gail Gerhart, quoted in Gibson, p10.

18 Patrick Bond (2006) *Talk Left, Walk Right: South Africa's Frustrated Global Reforms*, Scottsville: UKZN Press.

19 Harry Boyte (2008) The John Dewey Lecture, Minneapolis: University of Minnesota.

20 Jean Bayart (2005) *The Illusion of Identity*, Chicago: University of Chicago Press.

21 Hannah Arendt (1961), *Between Past and Future: Six Exercises in Political Thought*, New York: The Viking Press.

22 Ibid.

23 Ibid.

24 Gianna Pomata (1986) A common heritage: The historical memory of populism in Europe and the United States. In Harry C Boyte and Frank Riesman *The New Populism: The Politics of Empowerment*, Philadelphia: Temple University Press; Kundera, op.cit.

25 Arendt, op.cit.

26 Vaclav Havel (1989) The Power of the Powerless. In Jan Vladislav (Ed.) *Living in Truth*, London: Faber.

27   Ibid.

28   Arendt, op.cit.

29   Edward Said (2002) The public role of writers and intellectuals. In Helen Small (Ed.) *The Public Intellectual*, Oxford: Blackwell Publishers.

CHAPTER TWO   *The Transmission Lines*

1   RV Selope Thema 'The duty of Bantu intellectuals', *Umteteli wa Bantu*, 3 August 1929.

2   HIE Dhlomo 'Our Intellectuals', *Ilanga lase Natal*, 31 July 1943.

3   Edward Said (1975) *Beginnings: Intention and Method*, New York: Columbia University Press; Frank Kermode (1967) *The Sense of an Ending*, New York: Oxford University Press.

4   Kwame Nkrumah 'Africanism and culture', *Presence Africaine*, Vol. 17, No. 5, 1963.

5   'Xhosa nation prepares the way', *The Bantu World*, 15 October 1932.

6   'Anonymous' [definitely by HIE Dhlomo and Mark S Radebe], 'The Coming African Eisteddfod: Transvaal festival of all the Ttlents', *Umteteli wa Bantu*, 28 October 1933).

7   *UMbambatha Kamkhwatha*, foreword by Clement Martyn Doke, University of the Witwatersrand, 1949.

CHAPTER FOUR   *Africa in Europe, Egypt in Greece*

1   M Bernal (1987) *Black Athena: The Afroasiatic Roots of Classical Civilization. Vol. 1, The Fabrication of Ancient Greece 1785-1985*. London: Free Association Books and New Brunswick: Rutgers University Press.
– (1991) *Black Athena: The Afroasiatic Roots of Classical Civilization. Vol. 2, The Archaeological and Documentary Evidence*. London: Free Association Books and New Brunswick: Rutgers University Press.

– (2001) *Black Athena Writes Back*. Durham, NC and London: Duke University Press.

– (2006) *Black Athena: The Afroasiatic Roots of Classical Civilization. Vol.3, The Linguistic Evidence*. London: Free Association Books and New Brunswick: Rutgers University Press.

CHAPTER FIVE   *Unconquered and Insubordinate*

1   Meg Samuelson (2007) *Remembering the Nation, Disremembering Women? Stories of the South African Transition*. Scottsville: University of KwaZulu-Natal Press.

2   Wendy Isaack (2006) Deferred and disremembered: sexual violence against women in 'post-conflict' South Africa. LLM Dissertation. Belfast: Transitional Justice Institute, Universityof Ulster.

3   Phyllis Jordan (1984) 'Black womanhood and national liberation', *Sechaba*. December: 3–15.

4   Bunie Matlanyane Sexwale (1994) 'The politics of gender training', *Agenda* 23: 57–63.

5   Zoë Wicomb (2000) *David's Story*. Roggebaai: Kwela; Pumla Dineo Gqola (2004) 'As if this burden disguised as honour did not weigh heavily on her heart': Black women, struggle iconography and nation in South African literature', *AlterNation*. 11.1: 44–70.

6   Phyllis Jordan (1984) 'Black womanhood and national liberation', *Sechaba*. December: 3–15; Shireen Hassim (2006) *Women's Organizations and Democracies in South Africa: Contesting Authority*. Madison, WI: University of Wisconsin Press

7   Patricia McFadden (1997) 'The Challenges and Prospects of an African Women's Movement in the 21st Century', *Women in Action*. 1.

8   Patricia McFadden (2002) 'Intellectual Politics and Radical Feminist Praxis', *Feminist Africa*. 1: 86–90.

9   Shireen Hassim (2006) *Women's Organizations and Democracies in South Africa: Contesting Authority*. Madison, WI: University of Wisconsin Press.

10   Ibid.

11   Ibid.

12   Jacklyn Cock (1994) *Colonels and Cadres: War and Gender in South Africa*. Oxford: Oxford University Press.

13   Marja Anderton (1994) Review of Phyllis Ntantala's 'A life's mosaic', *Feminist Review*. 46: 101-103.

14   Margaret Lenta (2004) Review of 'Women Writing Africa: The Southern Region', *English in Africa*. 31.1: P.149.

15   Margaret Daymond, Dorothy Driver, Sheila Meintjes, Leloba Molema, Chiedza Musengezi, Margie Orford and Nobantu Rasebotsa (2003) *Women Writing Africa: The Southern Region*. New York: Feminist Press and Johannesburg: Wits University Press.

16   Margaret Lenta (2004) Review of 'Women Writing Africa: The Southern Region', *English in Africa*. 31.1: P.151.

17   Nomboniso Gasa (Ed.) (2007) *Basus' iimbokodo, bawel' imilambo: Women in South African History*. Cape Town: HSRC Press; Judith Lütge Coullie (Ed.) (2004) *The Closest of Strangers: South African Women's Life Writing*. Johannesburg: Wits University Press; Marja Anderton (1994) Review of Phyllis Ntantala's *A Life's Mosaic. Feminist Review*. 46: 101-103; Diana Russell (Ed.) (1989) *Lives of Courage: Women for a New South Africa*. New York: Basic Books.

18   Phyllis Jordan (1984) 'Black womanhood and national liberation', *Sechaba*. December: 3–15.

19   Cf. Pumla Dineo Gqola (2001) 'Contradictory locations: Black women and the discourse of the Black Consciousness Movement (BCM) in South Africa', *Meridians: Feminism, Race, Transnationalism*. 2.1: 130-152; Kimberley A Yates and Pumla Dineo Gqola (1998) 'This little bit of madness: Mamphela Ramphele on being black and transgressive', *Agenda*. 37: 90-95.

20   Susan Andrade (2002) 'Gender and "the public sphere" in Africa: writing women and rioting women', *Agenda*. 54: 45.

21 Judith Lütge Coullie (Ed.) (2006) *Selves in Question: Interviews on Southern African Autobiography*. Honolulu: University of Hawaii Press.

22 Margaret Daymond (1993) 'Seizing meaning: Language and ideology in the autobiographies of Ellen Kuzwayo and Emma Mashinini', *Journal of Literary Studies*. 9: 24-35; Dorothy Driver (1989) 'Reconstructing the self: Black women writers and the autobiographical text', in Rosalie Breitenbach (Ed.) *Journeys of Discovery: A Collection of Letters*. Grahamstown: 1820 Foundation.

23 Barbara-Anne Boswell (2010) 'Black South African Women Writers: Narrating the Self, Narrating the Nation', Unpublished PhD Dissertation, University of Maryland, College Park.

24 Bessie Head (1984) Foreword to Ellen Kuzwayo (1984) *Call me woman*. Braamfontein: Ravan.

25 Kate McKinnell (1987) 'Overwhelming tide of recognition continues for Ellen', *The Star*, 9 April 1987.

26 Gabeba Baderoon (2006) 'I forget to look', in *A Hundred Silences*. Roggebaai: Kwela.

27 Within literary studies, this is a significant body of work on BC literature, the writing of nationalism and gender in South African literature, departures in contemporary literature, representations and erasure of Black women in literature, activist women's biographies, etc (cf. Dorothy Driver, Desiree Lewis, JoAnne Prins, Pumla Dineo Gqola, Meg Samuelson, etc). Cf. also Nthabiseng Motsemme's significant oeuvre on women's testimonies at the TRC, as well as JoAnne Prins's work in the same field, Helen Bradford's, Patricia van der Spuy's and Yvette Abrahams's work on historiography and the gendering of South Africa's past, and Sheila Meintjes, Shireen Hassim, Nomboniso Gasa, Elaine Salo and Kimberley Yates on women's movements specifically.

28 Barbara Boswell (2006) 'Gender debate should shift from mean to meaningful', *Mail & Guardian*, 17-23 February, archived at http://www.mg.co.za/articlePage.

aspx?articleid=265003&area=/insight/insight__comment_
and_analysis/ (accessed 22 February 2006)

29   Ibid.

30   Gabeba Baderoon (2004) Oblique Figures:
Representations of Islam in South African Media and Culture.
Unpublished PhD thesis, University of Cape Town.

CHAPTER SIX   *Identity, Politics and the Archive*

1   Ronald Dworkin (2000) *Sovereign Virtue*, Cambridge:
Harvard University Press: 485, fn. 1. Note that Dworkin's
definition allows that the ethical might subsume the moral –
it might be best to lead a life in which you treat others as they
should be treated.

2   John Stuart Mill *On Liberty*. In John M Robson (Ed.) *The
Collected Works of John Stuart Mill*, vol. 18, Toronto: University
of Toronto Press, 1963–1991), 270.

3   Charles Taylor (1994) *Multiculturalism*: *Examining the
Politics of Recognition*, ed. Amy Gutmann, Princeton, NJ:
Princeton University Press, 1994), 36. Cf. Axel Honneth (1995)
The Struggle for Recognition, Cambridge, Mass: MIT Press.

4   Arjun Appadurai (2006) *Fear of Small Numbers: An
Essay on the Geography of Anger*, Durham and London: Duke
University Press, p. 3.

5   http://www.etymonline.com/index.php?term=statistics
accessed 6 July 2006.

6   See Eugen Weber (1991) 'Who Sang the Marseillaise,' in
My France. Politics, Culture, Myth, Cambridge, MA: Belknap
Press, 92-102.

7   Linda Colley (1992) *Britons: Forging the Nation, 1707-
1837*, London: Yale University Press.

8   «L'oubli, et je dirai même l'erreur historique, sont un
facteur essentiel de la création d'une nation, et c'est ainsi
que le progrès des études historiques est souvent pour la
nationalité un danger. » Ernest Renan «*Qu'est-ce qu'une*

nation?» 1882 as found at http://ourworld.compuserve.com/ homepages/bib_lisieux/nation02.htm July 2, 2006.

9 « l'essence d'une nation est que tous les individus aient beaucoup de choses en commun, et aussi que tous aient oublié bien des choses.» Ernest Renan «*Qu'est-ce qu'une nation?*» 1882 as found at http://ourworld.compuserve.com/ homepages/bib_lisieux/nation02.htm July 2, 2006.

10 «Une nation est une âme, un principe spirituel. Deux choses qui, à vrai dire, n'en font qu'une, constituent cette âme, ce principe spirituel. L'une est dans le passé, l'autre dans le présent. L'une est la possession en commun d'un riche legs de souvenirs ; l'autre est le consentement actuel, le désir de vivre ensemble, la volonté de continuer à faire valoir l'héritage qu'on a reçu indivis. L'homme, Messieurs, ne s'improvise pas. La nation, comme l'individu, est l'aboutissant d'un long passé d'efforts, de sacrifices et de dévouements. Le culte des ancêtres est de tous le plus légitime; les ancêtres nous ont faits ce que nous sommes. Un passé héroïque, des grands hommes, de la gloire (j'entends de la véritable), voilà le capital social sur lequel on assied une idée nationale.» Ernest Renan «*Qu'est-ce qu'une nation?*» 1882 as found at http://ourworld.compuserve.com/homepages/bib_lisieux/ nation04.htm July 2, 2006

11 Pankaj Mishra 'The Invention of the Hindu,' *Axess http:// www.axess.se/english/2004/02/theme_inventionhindu.php* July 17, 2006

CHAPTER EIGHT *Why Archive Matters*

1 This essay is based on research and debate undertaken initially in the Constitution of Public Intellectual Life Project, University of the Witwatersrand, and subsequently in the NRF research initiative in Archive and Public Culture at the University of Cape Town. Thanks are due to the Nelson Mandela Foundation for permission to incorporate into this essay materials and ideas formed in collaboration with

Verne Harris and originally presented in texts written for the Foundation. The present essay has roots in various bodies of work, some of which is collaborative, notably CA Hamilton *et al* (2005) for the Nelson Mandela Foundation, *A Prisoner in the Garden: Opening Nelson Mandela's Prison Archive*, Johannesburg: Penguin; CA Hamilton (2009) Uncertain citizenship and public deliberation in post-apartheid South Africa, *Social Dynamics*; C Hamilton, B Mbenga and R Ross 'The Production of Pre-industrial South African History'. In C Hamilton, B Mbenga and R Ross (Eds.) (2010) *Cambridge History of South Africa: From Earliest Times to 1885*, vol. 1, pp 1-62.

2   This argument is more fully developed in C Hamilton (2009) 'Uncertain citizenship and public deliberation in post-apartheid South Africa', *Social Dynamics*, vol.35, 2, September 2009, pp.355-374.

3   A Mbembe (2001) *On the Postcolony*, Berkeley: University of California Press.

4   Readers who are interested in exploring the theoretical developments around archive, and the debates within them, should track the impact of J Derrida (1995) *Archive Fever: A Freudian Impression*, trans. Eric Prenowitz, Chicago and London: University of Chicago Press; M Foucault's contributions in *The Archaeology of Knowledge and the Discourse on Language*, New York: Harper and Row, 1972; and M de Certeau's critique in *On the Writing of History*, New York: Columbia University Press, 1988. The first substantive South African engagement with the implications of these kinds of interventions appeared in the 2002 collection of essays, *Refiguring the Archive*, eds. CA Hamilton, V Harris, Jane Taylor, Michele Pickover, Graeme Reid and Razia Saleh, Dordrecht and Cape Town: Kluwer and David Philip, 2002. See also the work of the Archive and Public Culture Research Initiative, University of Cape Town, www.apc.uct.ac.za, notably the project on 'The Life of the Archive'. Also see C Hamilton 'The Public Life of an Archive: Archival Biography as Methodology', paper first presented to the CRESC Conference

on Archives and Reusing Qualitative Data: Theory, Methods and Ethics across the Disciplines, seminar on Epistemology of Archive, University of Sussex, November 2008.

5   See the text of Jacques Derrida's 1998 seminar in South Africa reproduced in Hamilton *et al* (Eds.) *Refiguring the Archive*, 38-80 alternate pp. only.

6   V Harris, 'An exercise in forgetting: Remembering the unfinished business of the TRC', first published in the newspaper *The Natal Witness*, 26 September 2002 and later reproduced in V Harris, (2007) *Archives and Justice: A South African Perspective*, Chicago: Society of American Archivists: 394-397.

7   These points are more fully developed in C Hamilton, B Mbenga and R Ross 'The Production of Pre-industrial South African History'. In C Hamilton, B Mbenga and R Ross (Eds.) (2010) *Cambridge History of South Africa: From Earliest Times to 1885*, vol. 1, p 1-62.

8   See the project 'Construing an Archive: The Material Record of the Thukela-Mzimkhulu Region, c.1730-1910', C Hamilton and N Leibhammer, www.apc.uct.ac.za.

9   See Hamilton, 'The Public Life of the Archive'.

10   See B Peterson (2000) *Monarchs, Missionaries and African Intellectuals: African Theatre and the Unmaking of Colonial Marginality*, Johannesburg: Wits University Press.

11   These very same features did, of course, make such texts available to local language publics.

12   These points are more fully developed in Hamilton, Mbenga and Ross, 'The Production of the Pre-industrial Past'.

13   Amartya Sen (1999) *Development as Freedom*, Oxford: Oxford University Press.

14   United Nations, Department of Social and Economic Affairs, Measures for the Economic Development of Underdeveloped Countries, 1951, p.15 cited in Escobar, p.4.

15   A Escobar (1995) *Encountering Development: The Making and Unmaking of the Third World*, Princeton: Princeton University Press.

16   I Chipkin (2007) *Do South Africans Exist? Nationalism, Democracy and the Identity of the People*, Johannesburg: Witwatersrand University Press, p.2.

17   X Mangcu 'Public Deliberation and Political Culture: Freeing up the South African Archive', opening address to the SAHA Workshop 'Memory, Heritage and the Public Interest', November 2006, Johannesburg. Available on www.public-conversations.org.za.

18   A Coombes (2004) *Visual Culture and Public Memory in a Democratic South Africa*, Johannesburg: Witwatersrand University Press.

19   See for example Zizi Kodwa, Comment: A Brood of Fangless Vipers, *Mail & Guardian*, 12-19 May 2006.

20   Summary and translation of Jacob Zuma's speech to his supporters, Nomfundo Xulu, Johncom Digital, Media Division.

21   Sipho Seepe, After Eight Debate, SABC, Monday 4 September 2006.

22   Nancy Fraser effectively exposes the way in which these kinds of tactics were used to discredit the testimony of Anita Hill in the hearings to confirm Clarence Thomas as a Supreme Court Justice of the USA (see her 'Sex, Lies and the Public Sphere: Some Reflections on the Confirmation of Clarence Thomas', *Critical Enquiry*, 1992, 18, 3:595612).

23   This section of my argument draws on Hamilton, 'Uncertain citizenship and public deliberation in post-apartheid South Africa', *Social Dynamics*, vol.35, 2, September 2009.

24   Jill Bennet (2005) *Empathic Vision: Affect, Trauma, and Contemporary Art*, Stanford: Stanford University Press.

25   Hamilton, 'Uncertain citizenship'. The work of Michael Warner provides an entry point into the notion of public subjectivity and the desire to participate vicariously in public bodies through certain kinds of media genres (M Warner (2002) *Publics and Counterpublics*, New York: Zone Books).

26   Nelson Mandela Foundation, *A Prisoner in the Garden: Opening Nelson Mandela's Prison Archive*, Johannesburg:

Penguin, 2005. I draw heavily in this section of the essay on examples cited in *A Prisoner in the Garden*.

27 *Archives at the Crossroads*, Open Report to the Minister of Arts and Culture from the Archival Conference, 'National System, Public Interest', 2007.

28 *A Prisoner in the Garden*, Chapter 1.

29 V Harris (2007) *Archives and Justice: A South African Perspective*, Chicago: Society of American Archivists, p. 4.

30 In identifying and arguing for these multiple sites of engaging archive, this essay responds to the challenge in the work of Premesh Lalu as to how, in the aftermath of the decentering of the archive as state institution, the archive works as a new kind of public 'institution' – as a space, not of authority, but of democratic debate (see his 'The Virtual Stampede for Africa: Digitisation, Postcoloniality and Archives of the Liberation Struggles in Southern Africa', paper presented to the SAHA workshop on 'Memory, Heritage and the Public Interest', November 2006).

INDEX

A

Abrahams, Peter viii, 27
affirmative action *see* black economic empowerment
African language families 60–61
    Afroasiatic 62–63
African language scholarship viii, 127
    Sotho 19–20
    Xhosa 19–21, 22, 24, 26–28, 30, 36, 40–43
    Zulu 20, 22, 28, 30, 36, 38–40, 42–43
    See also New African Movement
African National Congress (ANC) ix, 2–7, 9, 11–12, 21–25, 28–
    30, 32–34, 41, 51, 53, 55, 58, 68, 129, 132, 134–136, 139
    Umkhonto we Sizwe/armed struggle 52–53
    Youth League 3, 7, 33, 42
African nationalism ix, 5–6, 10, 19, 21–22, 24–25, 27–28, 107
    see also nationalism
African patriotism *see* African nationalism
African renaissance 8, 45
African unity 8, 22, 29
Africanism ix, 132, 134
afrocentrism x, 59
Andrade, Susan 78
anti-Semitism xi, 94
apartheid era 5–6, 8, 10, 43, 48, 50–52, 55, 57, 70–73, 79–80, 82,
    90, 108, 113, 120, 122, 124–131, 133, 135–137, 139–141
Arendt, Hannah 13–15
Azanian People's Organisation 6

B

Baderoon, Gabeba 82, 85
Bam, Brigalia Hlophe 76, 83
Barber, Benjamin 10

157

F

G

H

L

M

W

Z

Printed and bound by CPI Group (UK) Ltd, Croydon, CR0 4YY

09/06/2025